DAYTIME DIVAS

DAYTIME DIVAS

*The Dish on Dozens of
Daytime TV's Great Ladies*

KATHLEEN TRACY

RENAISSANCE BOOKS
Los Angeles

Library of Congress Catalog Card Number: 00-100887
ISBN: 1-58063-087-1

10 9 8 7 6 5 4 3 2 1

Design by Susan Shankin
Cover photos: (front, left three) Albert Ortega/Moonglow; (front, right) Barry Morgenstein; (back) Celebrity Photo Agency

Published by Renaissance Books
Distributed by St. Martin's Press
Manufactured in the United States of America
First Edition

CONTENTS

INTRODUCTION

They are the matriarchs of daytime serial drama. Love them or hate them, sympathize or empathize with them, cheer their attitudes or curse their wily ways, they are as much a mainstay of soapdom as star-crossed romance—and just as important to the unique flavor of the dramatic form we've come to know as soap opera. Their characters, often the most complex and compelling, propel the action and always command attention whenever they sweep onto the screen.

They are, quite simply, the divas of daytime.

Originally, the word *diva* simply referred to an opera singer. But over the years, the term has come to describe any grand lady—or any lady who acts too grand. Throughout the history of daytime drama there have been many actresses who have been categorized as examples of the latter. You know who they are. But just as many fall into the former category, and they may not be as well known to the newer generation of daytime fan.

Although all daytime dramas have their share of standard characters—the hunk, the scheming misfit, the sensitive man, the doomed lovers, the wacky character who provides comic relief, the ingenue, and the cad—the one character in particular who has come to epitomize the essence of soaps are the resident divas.

In a word, divas are indispensible. This is not to say that they cannot be written out, killed off, or criminally underused. But there are consequences, dahhh-ling. *As the World Turns* fans learned this lesson recently when leading diva Elizabeth Hubbard, frustrated over the direction her character had taken, opted not to renew her contract. Heads rolled, and once a new executive producer was in place, La Liz was lured back. And few fans of the show could deny that Oakdale was more than a trifle bland during her absence.

Although the stereotypic image of a diva is that of a lady of a certain age, being a diva has less to do with age than attitude—a manner, bearing, and temperament that only the most commanding, flamboyant, or dignified ladies of daytime can wear with authority.

The diva tends to always be in the middle of the action, whether working for the good of others or scheming for her personal gain. And although most divas do tend to be looking out for Number One (think *All My Children*'s Erica Kane), there are those who are endlessly selfless (think *Days of Our Lives*'s Marlena Evans). Some are boldly over the top (*Guiding Light*'s Reva Shayne), while others are more concerned with the bottom line (*The City*'s Sydney Chase).

From the boardroom to the bedroom, the grande dames of the soap opera world keep viewers tuning in by the millions to find out what's next in their bag of tricks. *Daytime Divas* examines the lives, loves, and lusts of these bigger-than-life characters, as well as the real-life escapades of their portrayers. With murder plots, illicit affairs, legal battles, and multiple trips down the aisle, sometimes it's hard to tell the actresses' offscreen antics from their onscreen action.

They scheme, dream, meddle, and manipulate. The best of them can incite fear with the mere arch of an eyebrow. They are the bold, beautiful, dynamic divas of daytime. And the following are arguably the best to ever grace TV screens.

JULIA BARR

From wild child to woman in red:
Julia Barr has portrayed Brooke English
for over twenty years.

Crowning Role: Brooke English on *All My Children*

Reign: 1976–81, 1982–present

Other Notable Roles: Reenie Szabo on *Ryan's Hope* (1976)

Character's Most Notable Pursuit: Becoming involved with Erica's discarded men

Character's Occupation: Magazine editor and director of a homeless shelter, the Brooke English House

Character's Full Name: Brooke English Cudahy Chandler Martin

Husbands: Tom Cudahy, Adam Chandler, and Tad Martin

Character's Diva-lution: As a teenager, Brooke English was a bad girl through and through. In 1976, she came to Pine Valley to live with her aunt, Phoebe Tyler. The change of scenery, however, didn't prevent her from continuing her affair with bad boy Benny Sago. Then the wild child offered herself up as Dan Kennicott's first sexual experience and from there became involved with Tom Cudahy, the object of desire of many Pine Valley women, including Erica Kane.

Erica eventually married Tom, but a few years after that, they divorced and he married Brooke, with whom he had a daughter, Laura. Brooke, now a reporter, ended their marriage in 1984 after learning that Tom and Erica had had a one-night stand.

In 1981, Brooke discovered that the woman she always believed to be her mother, Peg English, wasn't. Peg was revealed to be an international drug dealer. Go figure. Brooke's natural mother was a homeless woman. This discovery raised Brooke's social conscious-ness and got her involved with the plight of the homeless. A year later, Brooke's world was shattered when her daughter, Laura, was killed by a drunk driver.

Brooke's second marriage, to Adam Chandler, ended after Brooke learned that Adam had fathered a child with another woman.

In 1990, Brooke conceived a child with Tad Martin, who was then estranged from his true love, Dixie. Two years later, convinced that he had lost Dixie forever, Tad married Brooke and together they planned to raise their son, Jamie. Their marriage was short-lived, however, as Tad eventually found his way back to Dixie.

In 1996, Brooke fell in love with a brooding artist, Pierce Riley. Their engagement ended after his presumed-dead former lover resurfaced in Pine Valley. Brooke concentrated on raising her family, which now consisted of her son, Jamie, and her adopted daughter, Laura Kirk, once a homeless teenager.

After being one of only four survivors of a plane crash, Brooke teamed up with another survivor, Jim Thomasen, to uncover the truth behind the crash. Turns out Thomasen was a child pornographer who had taken X-rated pictures of Laura when she was a young child. Jim staged a kidnapping of Laura, then "rescued" her so that Brooke would become indebted to him. Brooke fell hook, line, and sinker. Jim also convinced Laura to leave town. Naturally, Brooke was mighty peeved when it came to light that Jim was a pornographer and was also responsible for the plane crash. During an angry confrontation, Brooke shot and killed him. She went on trial and was eventually acquitted.

Since then, she has been as busy as ever running her magazine and helping the homeless.

Of Special Note: Elissa Leeds originated the role of Brooke English in 1976. Barr took a fifteen-month hiatus in 1981 to tour with Katharine Hepburn and Dorothy Loudon in the national company of *West Side Waltz.* During that time, the role of Brooke was played by Harriet Hall.

Real-Life Soap Opera: Julia Barr grew up in Fort Wayne, Indiana, and attended college at Purdue University, where she appeared in such school productions as *Our Town, A Streetcar Named Desire,* and *Endgame.*

Her first soap job was on *Ryan's Hope.* When her role was written out, she segued into *All My Children* where she racked up seven Emmy nominations and took home the statuette twice. In addition to her work on the soap, Barr has also managed to maintain her ties to the theater, appearing in such productions as the Off-Broadway *Kerouac* and *Absurd Person Singular,* the first tour made up of daytime performers.

Barr is married to oral surgeon Dr. Richard Hirschlag. They have a teenage daughter, Allison.

Awards and Accolades: Barr has won two Emmy Awards for Outstanding Supporting Actress (1990 and 1998) out of seven nominations. She also received a *Soap Opera Digest* Award for Best Supporting Actress in 1990.

In April 1996, Barr was bestowed with the Women in Business Award for her work with helping homeless women.

Causes: Like her character, Julia has devoted much time to the issue of homelessness. She has been a spokesperson for the Company of Women, a national merchandise catalog whose proceeds help fund the Rockland Family Shelter. She has also been involved with First Step, a job readiness program, with the Coalition for the Homeless in New York City.

Div-o-Meter: 1—Barr is the classic anti-diva. A self-professed "jeans kind of girl," Julia would rather be rollerblading with her daughter than primping for her next close-up.

PATRICIA BARRY

Days of Our Lives' *Addie* competed
with her own daughter for the affections
of Doug Williams (Bill Hayes).

Crowning Role: Addie Olson Williams on *Days of Our Lives*

Reign: 1971–74

Other Notable Roles: Laurie James on *First Love* (a fifteen-minute
soap aired live from Philadelphia from July 1954 to December
1955); Viola Brewster on *For Richer, For Poorer* (1978); Peg English on
All My Children (1980–81); Sally Gleason on *Guiding Light* (1983–87);
and Isabelle Alden on *Loving* (1992–94)

What Patricia Says About Addie: "Macdonald Carey [who
played patriarch Tom Horton] had an absolute fit when I was cast as
his daughter because we had played love interests and contempo-
raries in other television series." Barry adds, however, "He got over
the shock."

Character's Most Notable Pursuit: Stealing her daughter's boyfriend

Character's Full Name: Addie Horton Olson Williams

Husbands: Ben Olson and Doug Williams

Character's Diva-lution: Addie Horton was one of five children born to Dr. Tom Horton and his wife, Alice. She married Ben Olson and they had a daughter, Julie.

In 1970, Addie was in Paris when Doug Williams arrived in Salem and became romantically involved with her daughter, Julie. Julie was then married to Scott Banning. Addie strongly disapproved of the affair and confronted Doug about it.

After Doug and Julie had a falling out, Addie brazenly began her own romance with Doug. Being a take-charge kind of gal, she proposed to him. He accepted, and they eloped—throwing Julie for just a little loop. Julie was thrown for an even bigger loop when Addie became pregnant and gave birth to a daughter, Hope.

After surviving a bout with leukemia, Addie was killed while saving Hope from being hit by an oncoming truck.

Of Special Note: Pat Huston originated the role of Addie Olson.

Real-Life Soap Opera: Patricia Barry grew up in Davenport, Iowa. Her father, a head surgeon at the famed Mayo Clinic, was a stickler about education. Although Patricia was a good student, her heart was in performing, specifically dancing, until a freak accident changed the course of her life.

"As a child, I started out dancing. Then I went to a party, at the country club, when I was about sixteen, and I was enamored of the golf caddy. The golf caddy and I were up on the stage goofing around. He poked me on my shoulder, and the next thing I knew I was sailing off the apron of the stage. I landed on my kneecap and destroyed it. I knew I could never be a professional dancer. But I consider that a very lucky break because I don't know if I could have endured the life of a dancer."

Rather than be daunted by her misfortune, Barry took up acting and after high school, attended Stevens College, in Columbia, Missouri, which had a well-regarded theater department, headed by the famous stage actress Maude Adams.

"By this time she was in her late seventies," Patricia recalls. "She was adorable and tiny. She wore these little boots and a three-cornered hat with a green veil and wore a cape. She wouldn't allow us to wear jeans. We had to wear skirts when we came to class. When she came in, we all stood up and curtsied to her. I consider that the most valuable training in the world that I could possibly have had at that age."

After seeing an ad in a theater trade paper, Barry got her first professional job as an assistant technical director during the summer between her freshman and sophomore years. Soon after, she appeared on Broadway for the first time and from there worked steadily in films.

Even though television was originally looked down on as a lesser art, Barry had no qualms about working in the new medium. Her first soap was, appropriately, *First Love,* a Philadelphia-based soap. She joined *Days of Our Lives,* mostly she says, because she wanted to spend more time with her daughter.

"My daughter Stephanie was in high school. I could no longer travel back and forth to New York, doing regional theater and tours. I had to have a steady schedule. I was a member of all these organizations and I wanted to concentrate on the mother/daughter activities.

"So I called Wes Kenney, who was the producer of *Days of Our Lives*. I had worked with him on *First Love*, the only soap I had done up to this point. I explained why I wanted to do a soap and he told me about a character on the show who was Julie's mother—the mother she hated."

The duration of the role was dictated by Barry. She explains, "I suggested to them that I would like to do the role for a couple of years until Stephanie entered college."

They agreed, and once Stephanie flew out of the nest, Barry moved on. Although she says Addie was by far her favorite character, she could never go back. "To bring her back as a twin or cousin would simply be unfair to the audience."

Since she left *Days*, Barry has continued dividing her acting time between films, primetime, theater, and soaps. *Guiding Light* fans will remember her as H. B. Lewis's gal pal, Sally Gleason. On *Loving*, she replaced Augusta Dabney as matriarch Isabelle Alden.

Awards and Accolades: Barry has been nominated for four Emmy Awards.

Div-o-Meter: 7—Although her career literally spans the age of soaps, Barry has never stayed in one role long enough to form the power foundation necessary to rise to the top of divadom.

JAIME LYN BAUER

As Y&R's *Lorie Brooks, Jaime Lyn Bauer raised the temperature of daytime.*

Crowning Role: Dr. Laura Horton on *Days of Our Lives*

Reign: 1993–present

Other Notable Roles: Lauralee "Lorie" Brooks on *The Young and the Restless* (1973–82)

Character's Occupation: Psychiatrist

Character's Most Notable Pursuit: Getting out of the mental hospital

Character's Full Name: Laura Ann Spencer Horton Horton

Husbands: Mickey Horton and Bill Horton

Character's Diva-lution: Laura Ann Spencer, who studied medicine at Johns Hopkins University, came to Salem as a psychiatric intern. She began dating doctor Bill Horton in 1967, but after he was diagnosed with tuberculosis, Bill abruptly left Salem. Laura began dating Bill's brother, Mickey, and they fell in love. When Bill finally returned, he learned that Laura and Mickey were engaged. Bill still loved Laura and was devastated when his brother married her.

Late one night at the hospital, a drunken Bill raped Laura. She never told anyone about the incident, including Bill, who had no memory of what had happened. So when she discovered she was pregnant, everyone assumed the baby—Michael William, born in September 1968—was Mickey's. But what Mickey didn't know was that he was sterile. Bill came across the test results showing his brother's infertility, recovered his memory, and figured out the truth. Of course, not wanting to be charged with rape, he kept mum.

When Bill got out of prison on a questionable manslaughter conviction, he still loved Laura, and despite the rape, it was obvious that she loved him, too. Meanwhile, Mickey cheated on Laura, but she wouldn't divorce him because she discovered he had a heart condition. When Mickey suffered a potentially fatal heart attack, it was Bill who operated on him and saved his life. Mickey subsequently suffered a stroke resulting in amnesia.

When Mickey disappeared from the hospital, Bill and Laura became closer, although they wouldn't sleep together until Mickey's fate had been determined. Eventually, Mickey was found on a farm and had no idea who Laura was. That being the case, they were divorced. At long last, Bill and Laura were reunited, and they married on December 4, 1974.

Their happiness was short-lived. When Mickey and Laura's son, Michael, was hurt in a farm accident and his true paternity was revealed, Mickey's memory suddenly came back. He was so outraged at the deceit that he tried to murder his brother and as a result was committed to Bayview Sanitarium.

Things remained rocky for Laura when she discovered that Bill was cheating on her with Kate Roberts. Even after he ended the affair, Laura couldn't bring herself to completely trust him and began to break down emotionally. She completely crumbled after her mother committed suicide, claiming to see the dead woman's ghost and hear her voice. Laura finally snapped and tried to kill herself, too. After he saved her life, Bill had Laura institutionalized, where she would remain for eighteen years in a catatonic state.

In 1993, Laura was finally released, although her mental health still seemed suspect. When she was caught forging prescriptions, Bill threatened to have her thrown back in the sanitarium if she didn't stop. After their son, Michael, promised to watch after his mom, Bill left Salem, and he and Laura divorced.

Of Special Note: Five different actresses—Floy Dean (1966), Susan Flannery (1966–75), Susan Oliver (1975–76), Rosemary Forsythe (1976–80), and Bauer—have played the role of Laura Horton. When *Days* producers decided to bring back the character of Laura in 1993, Rosemary Forsythe auditioned for the part, but didn't get the role.

Real-Life Soap Opera: Jaime Lyn Bauer was born in Phoenix, Arizona. Her dad was an airline pilot and her mom dabbled in singing, but the music stopped when her parents divorced when Jaime was just two. In order to put food on the table, her mom worked two jobs, meaning Jaime and her three siblings were often on their own—and often went without.

"I owned just five dresses, and when I was twelve had to keep house and cook for five people," Bauer says.

But the experience taught her some important life lessons. "All you really have is your integrity, your past is not an excuse for your present, hard work is rewarded, and don't ever lose your sense of humor."

Looking for a way to improve her lot, Bauer entered a Junior Miss Pageant, which led to her being a runner-up in the Miss Arizona Pageant. Encouraged by her success, Jaime Lyn dropped out of Phoenix Junior College after a year and a half and moved to Chicago where her grandmother lived. While earning her keep as a bookkeeper, Jaime began modeling and entered the Miss Illinois Pageant, where she was second runner-up. "I won the bathing suit part, but it was all politics," she says.

In what would prove to be typical early Bauer behavior, she impulsively moved to Los Angeles to be with her boyfriend. After they split up, however, Jaime suddenly had to fend for herself.

"I thought I could supplement my modeling income with acting," she recalls. "I was very lucky. I landed several television roles in my first month of trying and my acting career grew from there."

And it grew quickly. Within a few months, Jaime had to choose between two promising offers—a seven-year contract with Universal Studios as a contract player or a three-year contract with *The Young and the Restless*. Bauer chose the soap, which at the time she noted was the only daytime serial "without organ music."

As *Y&R*'s Lorie Brooks, Bauer raised daytime's temperature with storylines that included romancing a man who turned out to be her half-brother and causing her sister to have a nervous breakdown. Ironically, Bauer's real life was equally as complicated. By the time she was thirty-one, Bauer had been married twice, had a baby, suffered three miscarriages, and had been involved in some high profile relationships, including a romance with then-Fonz, Henry Winkler.

Her life turned around, however, when she met her second husband, Emmy Award–winning makeup artist Jeremy Swan, and converted to Catholicism. Enduring the ordeal that surrounded the birth of her son, Gabrielle, also matured Bauer. Bauer was forced to have her cervix sewn shut and be wheelchair-bound in order to bring the difficult pregnancy to term.

Bauer remained on *The Young and the Restless* for nine years, until 1982—the same year she posed nude for a *Playboy* pictorial featuring the women of daytime television. From there she went primetime, starring in the evening soap *Bare Essence,* which revolved around the backstabbing world of the perfume industry and starred another soap veteran, Genie Francis. The series was pulled after a few months.

Bauer made a brief return to *Y&R* in 1984, then spent the next few years working in theater. In 1986, not long after her second child, a daughter, was born, her son had a grand mal seizure and was eventually diagnosed with epilepsy. Bauer put her career on hold for the next four years until his condition stabilized. Her comeback role was in a movie of the week, followed by guest spots on *Knot's Landing* and *Young Riders.*

In October 1993, Bauer made a triumphant return to daytime as the nearly forgotten Dr. Laura Horton. She has been spicing up the town of Salem ever since.

Causes: The cause closest to Jaime's heart is educating people about epilepsy, an affliction that she is intimately familiar with because one of her three children suffers from the neurological disorder.

"My child's doctor said he had a seizure disorder. It was two years after that when I finally learned it meant he had epilepsy—epilepsy simply means recurring seizures. It was like a lightbulb going on."

When she tried to learn about epilepsy, however, she hit a wall. "I searched for information but found very little under *seizure disorder.* Try looking that up in the phone book! However, when I looked under *epilepsy,* I discovered the Epilepsy Foundation in Los Angeles.

They sent me the kind of information I'd spent so much time searching for and I sat my family down and read it to them.

"I can't say they were especially thrilled by the whole thing. But families really do need to educate themselves. I always encourage parents to do whatever they can to find other parents for advice and support. Women with the disorder can also benefit from sharing experiences and information with other women who have seizures."

Bauer admits that early on she felt very much alone, in part because, "As the mother of a child with a chronic illness, you also have to be a master planner, timekeeper, and, hardest of all, enforcer of rules. We're also the ones that manage the child's medical tests, doctor visits, and medication schedules. We fight the battles with the school, the sports department—anyone and everyone who thinks they know what's best for our child."

For years, Bauer kept her son's condition a secret, but that changed in 1995 when the Epilepsy Foundation of America asked her to be their spokesperson. Jaime Lyn accepted the offer and made the decision to go public, amid strong resistance from her loved ones.

"My family wanted epilepsy kept within the family, where it had always been," notes Bauer. She says that her son who has the disorder "freaked out and my husband argued with me about going public. The other children cried and pleaded with me. It broke my heart.

"But I said, 'Guys, if I stay silent then we keep him a victim forever. Our only hope is to bring it into the light.'"

Bauer's decision was two-fold—to educate people about the affliction itself and to acknowledge the strain that epilepsy—which afflicts more than two million Americans—can place on families and relationships. Although it is not an uncommon disorder, Bauer notes that epilepsy has "been pushed underground due to shame and superstition and ignorance."

The key to understanding epilepsy, Bauer has learned, is education. And the key to helping epileptics is to give them a support system. (For more information, contact the Epilepsy Foundation at 1-800-332-1000 and ask for the office nearest you. Or check the foundation's Web site: www.efa.org.)

Looking back, Jaime Lyn remains convinced that her decision to go public was the right one. "There has been tremendous healing in our relationships with one another and more openness. I pray for the day when they'll be able to talk openly about epilepsy with anyone. It'll take time. We got started late because we had so many secrets. But what's happened so far is nothing short of a miracle."

Most Notable Real-Life Diva Moment: Her secret three-month 1977 marriage to a psychologist, a union she compares to "biting into a delicious-looking cream cake and finding it tasted like dust."

Trivia: Perhaps Bauer's most famous onscreen liaison was in a steamy *Young and the Restless* shower scene with a newcomer named Tom Selleck.

Div-o-Meter: 3—Although she gets points for sheer longevity and the audaciousness of her characters, it would literally go against her belief system to indulge in divadom offcamera.

How to Be a Diva

Every true diva knows that it's all in the attitude—you can't get that in an instruction manual. If you have to ask, you probably don't stand a chance. For those aspiring to divadom, however, here are a few tips to get you started:

1. Hire a maid. Divas don't do housework.

2. Marry rich. Poverty does not become a diva.

3. Go all out. Whoever said, "Everything in moderation," wasn't a diva.

4. Be mysterious. Divas never reveal all their secrets.

5. Never let them see you sweat. Maintain grace under pressure at all times.

6. Never let them see you *in* sweats. If you're going to be a diva, dress the part.

7. Speak loudly and carry a big stick. Divas are not known for their meekness.

8. Be in a league all your own. Divas don't run with a pack.

9. Emulate Loretta Young. Dramatic entrances and exits will enhance your legend and give that needed panache.

10. Don't believe it's a man's world. Divas don't *need* men, but they may want one (or several) around to do their bidding.

11. Great hair. Never underestimate the power coif.

12. Throw away this list. Divas make their own rules.

LESLIE CHARLESON

Leslie Charleson has earned four Emmy nominations for her role as Monica Quartermaine on General Hospital.

Crowning Role: Monica Quartermaine on *General Hospital*

Reign: 1977–present

Other Notable Roles: Iris Donnelly on *Love Is a Many Splendored Thing* (1967–70)

Character's Most Notable Pursuit: Balancing the nonstop action of her private life with running the hospital and dealing with it all through humor

Character's Occupation: Surgeon and chief of staff at General Hospital

Character's Full Name: Monica Bard Webber Quartermaine

Husbands: Dr. Jeff Webber and Alan Quartermaine

Character's Diva-lution: Monica Bard grew up in an orphanage, but when she was seventeen she was taken in by Dr. Gail Adamson. Monica was a gifted student and went on to become a top medical student. After finishing medical school, Monica, who by then was married to Jeff Webber, began working at General Hospital as an intern. Soon after, she began having an affair with her husband's brother, Rick Webber. She and Jeff split up as a result. When he found out his brother was the one who had come between him and his wife, Jeff tried to kill himself.

Guilt-ridden, Monica ended her relationship with Rick and went back to Jeff. Too much damage had been done, however, and they divorced. Not long afterward, Monica fell in love with Alan Quartermaine, and they were married. Although they remain together, their marriage has had its ups and downs. During one low period when she and Alan were separated, Rick came back to town and Monica had a brief affair with him. The fling ended when she and Alan reconciled. In a case of notorious soap opera bad timing, Monica discovered she was pregnant (does nobody on soaps use birth control?). The stress of believing she was carrying Rick's child took its toll on Monica, who went into labor prematurely. While giving birth, she confessed to Dr. Lesley Webber, Rick's wife, that the baby was Rick's. Although initial blood tests seemed to confirm that, it was later proven that the child was truly Alan's.

But in a case of what's good for the goose is not good for the gander, when Monica learned that Alan had an affair with Susan Moore, who in turn had given birth to his child, Jason, she filed for divorce. When Susan died, however, Monica took Jason in and raised him as her own child. She and Alan also reconciled, as soap couples are wont to do.

Besides her marital woes, Monica has had other dramas, such as being reunited with her daughter, Dawn, whom she had given up for adoption years earlier, only to have Dawn up and die. Monica also battled, and beat, breast cancer.

Although Monica has lived a fairly law-abiding life, at least by soap standards, she did kidnap a former lover, Pierce Dorman, after he falsely sued her for sexual harassment. He, too, got his comeuppance by dying.

In recent years, Monica has helped Alan overcome an addiction to painkillers, she and Alan have adopted another child, and she has risen through the hospital ranks to become the chief of staff.

Of Special Note: Patsy Rahn (1976–77) originated the role of Monica.

Favorite Storyline: Battling breast cancer. "When I started in daytime," Charleson notes, "we were never allowed to do any stories that were political or topical. You stayed in the middle of America, and you never stepped on a toe. I've always thought that wasn't right, because we have an audience five days a week, year in and year out, where people really do listen and believe. If we can educate them, it is all the better."

In fact, the breast cancer story arc was actually Leslie's idea. "I thought it might be interesting for my character. After a while on a soap, you have to do more than just have affairs."

Real-Life Soap Opera: Leslie Charleson was born in Kansas City, Missouri. After graduating from Bennett College in Millbrook, New York, where Leslie was voted the outstanding theater arts student of her class, she moved to New York City, where she studied with famed acting teacher Uta Hagen.

One of Leslie's first roles was in a short-lived daytime drama called *Flame in the Wind* on ABC. The soap later changed its name to *A Time for Us.* After that, she was cast as Iris Donnelly on *Love Is a*

Many Splendored Thing. Charleson recalls that there was a point where Iris was "blind, pregnant, and dying—all at once." That, truly, is the stuff soap operas are made of.

After leaving that show, Charleson went to Los Angeles, where she appeared as a guest star in dozens of television series. She also became a familiar face in many national commercials and costarred in several films and plays. But her career-making role has been Monica Quartermaine, who has been a fixture on *General Hospital* for more than twenty years.

When she is not busy saving lives and trying to maintain her own on the soap, Charleson can often be found riding and showing her prized possession, an Andalusian horse named Andarra.

Awards and Accolades: For her role as Monica Quartermaine, Charleson has been nominated for four Emmys in the Outstanding Actress category (1980, 1982, 1983, and 1995). She has also been nominated for four *Soap Opera Digest* Awards, three for Outstanding Actress (1986, 1988, and 1990) and once for Outstanding Supporting Actress (1993).

Causes: Leslie is an active spokesperson for breast cancer, cystic fibrosis, and AIDS-related charities.

Trivia: As a guest star on *Happy Days,* Charleson gave Ron Howard his first onscreen kiss.

Div-o-Meter: 4—Although a fan favorite, Leslie (like Monica) is too good-natured to rank very high on the Diva scale.

JEANNE COOPER

*Jeanne Cooper plays Kay Chancellor,
the terror of Genoa City.*

Crowning Role: Katherine "Kay" Chancellor on *The Young and the Restless*

Reign: 1973–present

What Jeanne Says About Katherine: "She's so vulnerable. With all of her wealth and all of her finesse and her elegance Kay is always shoved to the ground and has to pick herself up—although she hits the ground without looking like she hit the ground and that, I think, is what everybody would like to do."

Character's Most Notable Pursuit: Resiliency

Character's Occupation: Owner of Chancellor Industries

Character's Full Name: Katherine Shepherd Reynolds Chancellor Thurston Sterling

Husbands: Gary Reynolds, Phillip Chancellor II, Derek Thurston, and Rex Sterling (aka Brian Romalotti)

Character's Diva-lution: Kay Chancellor has been the terror of Genoa City for decades. She became one of its richest residents after inheriting her husband's fortune. Phillip Chancellor II died as a result of injuries suffered in a car accident that occurred with Kay at the wheel. She had lost control in despair after Phillip announced he was in the process of divorcing her so he could marry Kay's soon-to-be-ex-friend, Jill Foster, who happened to be pregnant with Phillip's child.

On his deathbed, Phillip did marry Jill, but the ceremony was later deemed illegal because his divorce from Kay wasn't final. After Jill gave birth to Phillip III, Kay did her damnedest to get custody of the child. She didn't succeed, but she did forge a familial relationship with him. Tragically, young Phillip had a drinking problem and he was killed when he crashed his car while drunk.

Everywhere Kay turned, it seemed as if Jill was there waiting to stab her in the heart—and vice versa—such as when Jill briefly "married" Kay's son Brock, a minister. (The ceremony was not performed legally.)

And if it wasn't Jill causing her grief, it was the men she picked. Derek Thurston was a con artist who was only interested in Kay's money, but she didn't realize that until after she married him. Kay's rival for Derek's affections was none other than Jill. Kay was so hellbent on keeping Derek from Jill that she bribed him into remaining in the loveless marriage for one year.

Then there was her romance with Rex Sterling, a charming ex-con, that led to marriage, divorce, and remarriage. Rex, who was revealed to be Danny Romalotti's father, Brian, had reformed, and things actually seemed to be working out the second time around—until the night Rex walked in on Norman Peterson stealing jewelry from Katherine's safe. Caught in the act, Norman shot and killed Rex, leaving Kay absolutely devastated.

Perhaps Katherine's biggest battle, though, was with herself. It took her years to finally admit she was out of control and to stand in front of an Alcoholics Anonymous group and announce, "My name is Kay and I'm an alcoholic."

Even sober, Kay still never misses an opportunity to tweak Jill. Ironically, their feud happens to be the most stable and consistent relationship of Katherine's life.

Favorite Storyline: "I loved the one particular moment where Katherine is dumped again on a cruise ship and decides she'll jump overboard, and she's picked up by this South American rebel, or Central American rebel, and she was captive in the jungle with nothing but her jewels, with a lovely Latino guy, but they began to quarrel and take on the aspects of life and it became like a Lucy/Desi thing, because she would get so furious and she would speak these certain words in Spanish and he would get furious with her and speak certain words in English and the rest was in Spanish. We were interpreting for the audience at times. It was so delightful and such fun."

Of Special Note: In one of the more daring storylines in the history of *The Young and the Restless,* Kay Chancellor dabbled in lesbianism in 1977. But the ahead-of-its-time plotline was quickly squelched after viewers voiced strong disapproval.

Real-Life Soap Opera: Wilma Jeanne Cooper was born on October 25, 1929, in the town of Taft, California, not far from Bakersfield. Both her parents were born on a Cherokee Indian reservation in Oklahoma and worked in the oil business after settling in California.

Jeanne attended East Bakersfield High School and remembers the experience with nostalgic fondness. "I fell in love with the theater there! And Bakersfield Community theater . . . I played Rose in *Blithe Spirit* and got great reviews—and smoked a cigarette in the play. The principal saw it and she asked if there was any way I couldn't smoke a cigarette on that stage. Beautiful memories."

Later, Jeanne attended the College of the Pacific and performed in the Civic Light Opera Company and Revue Theater in Stockton. She graduated from the famed Pasadena Playhouse School.

Jeanne learned the ropes by working constantly. She says, "Yeah, the Golden Age of Television . . . from *Hallmark Hall of Fame, Playhouse 90, Bonanza, Perry Mason, Twilight Zone, Dick Tracy,* to *Zulus.* You name it, I appeared in 400 episodics! Those were fun.

"When I was doing *Wagon Train,* there was an adorable little girl on the show and her name was Melody Thomas," who would become famous on soaps as Melody Thomas Scott. "Oh God it all comes back to me, I've done so much!"

Between the late 1950s and early 1970s, Cooper also worked steadily in films, appearing in such efforts as *Sweet Hostage, Kansas City Bomber, The Glory Guys, Shame, House of Women, Intruder, Plunder Road, Five Steps to Danger, The Man from the Alamo,* and *Red Nightmare.*

So when she was cast as Katherine Chancellor, Cooper brought to the part a full career of experience and helped make *Y&R* the number-one rated soap for more than a decade. She was also very vocal about the reasons the show began slipping in the mid 1990s.

"For a while, *Y&R* was all about twenty year olds, who," she added dryly, "contrary to network opinion do not run the world, and we didn't see much of Katherine. Everybody blamed the O. J. Simpson trial for falling ratings. Bull——! Viewers dropped out because we were selling nothing but sex and extreme youth. We became very Calvin Klein–ish, we started competing with porno and that doesn't work with daytime viewers. They want to use their imaginations. They don't want to see anybody's naked butt."

Despite having logged more than twenty-five years on the soap, Cooper believes there are still great storylines to be had. A recent story development suggested by Cooper herself, has Katherine raising a runaway granddaughter, Mackenzie. She had said, "Fifty percent of all children are being raised by grandparents, you know. I really would love to see Katherine have to take on the responsibility of raising a child and being taught that child's eye because I personally am seeing it through my grandsons, Weston and Harrison, who are part-time residents of Grandma."

Although some actors exude false modesty when asked about their careers, Jeanne is candid about the legacy she feels she will leave behind. "Respect. I've made other actors of repute realize and recognize the quality and integrity of a lot of actors in daytime. I think I set the standard by which people are measured."

And as for whether she has been overlooked for an Emmy, Cooper notes, "Anybody who's lived through forty years in this business should take home a statue."

Awards and Accolades: For four consecutive years from 1989 to 1992, Jeanne was nominated for a Daytime Emmy as Outstanding Actress. In 1989, she won the *Soap Opera Digest* Award as Outstanding Actress and also received the magazine's Editor's Award that same year. Cooper was named Woman of the Year by the Pasadena Playhouse Alumni and Associates in 1989, and *Soap Opera Update* honored her with its MVP Award in 1990. Jeanne was also the proud recipient of the First Americans in the Arts Award for Best Actress in a Daytime Drama in 1998.

Causes: Working with the terminally ill. Cooper says she keeps them "motivated and helps them use that inner light and soul we don't call upon often enough."

Also, in 1987, Cooper established the Katherine Chancellor Society, a different kind of fan club. To join, each member must promise to contribute to society, whether through a church, charity, or community organization—and then report their good deeds back to Cooper.

Jeanne also donates her time to several charities, hospitals, and organizations, including the Humane Society of Hawaii, Greenpeace, the National Wildlife Association, Children's Hospital of Toronto, Children's Cancer Research (London), House of Hope (San Diego, California), and Drive by Agony (Lynwood, California).

Feuds: Okay, so maybe it's not a real-life feud but the epic twenty-four-year squabble between Kay Chancellor and Jill Abbott has truly taken on a life of its own. "We're talking about the longest battle in television history," Cooper points out. "Actually, it's the longest story-line and this to me is amazing.

"The truth is, Kay loves Jill very much and Jill loves her very much. The conflict is the whole thing and neither one of them has taken this up with the other, they're so busy as to who did what to who, who interjected what. Katherine was so vulnerable at the time so anything could have happened and Jill was young and dumb, you know, she couldn't even get a decent manicure," she laughs. "So the color is really there's a lot of love/hate that goes on between them.

"The audience loves Jill and Kay, and no matter what age, they totally understand them. Even today, you got the young faction, and the eighteen and nineteen year olds, and they all love Kay and Jill. They love it. And their mothers love it and their grandmothers love it."

Most Notable Real-Life Diva Moment: Jeanne Cooper is nothing if not a straight shooter, unafraid to let her real life seep over onto her screen world. So in 1984, when she decided it was time for a nip-and-tuck, Jeanne suggested that her character, Kay, follow suit. More than just writing the cosmetic surgery into the story, Cooper allowed actual footage of her operation to be aired on the show.

Likewise, it was well known to viewers that Katherine was a secret lush. What wasn't known is that Cooper herself was an alcoholic. So when she summoned the courage to acknowledge it and check into rehab, the writers had Katherine sober up as well.

"Katherine and I represent something I'm very proud of," Jeanne says with conviction. "We're showing mothers and grandmothers and—most importantly—kids that you don't have to sit on the porch and rock when you get old. You can still be on your feet fighting, improving your looks and conquering your problems."

Trivia: From her marriage to producer Harry Bernsen, Jeanne Cooper has three children, Corbin, Collin, and Caren. Corbin is well known to TV fans from his role as *L.A. Law*'s libidinous divorce attorney, Arnie Becker. Cooper earned an Emmy nomination for guest starring on *L.A. Law* as Arnie's mother.

Div-o-Meter: 10+—For someone who has lived the life she has, on- and offcamera, and remained a vibrant aspect of her show for a quarter-century, can there be any doubt?

Cooper's 25th Anniversary

In honor of Jeanne Cooper's longtime contribution to the continuing success of *The Young and the Restless,* the producers threw their star a much-deserved party. One of the highlights was a speech given by the soap's creator, William Bell: "Twenty-five years ago, on this date, Jeanne taped her very first show. Since then, my estimate is that she has appeared in over 3,000 episodes!"

Bell recounted the history of Cooper's character, including the tumultuous relationship between Kay and Jill, stating, "Eventually Kay would prevail on Jill to come and live with her and be her paid companion. That proved to be a very tragic mistake because Jill, in her innocence, ultimately married Kay's husband, which to this day is the basis of the hostility that exists between these two women. Something tragic and unexpected happened over the years; art imitating life . . . and life imitating art because during the telling of this story—possibly as a result of it—Jeanne had her own personal battle with the bottle. And the bottle won.

"I don't say this to embarrass Jeanne . . . but rather to show how her strength and determination over many many months helped her to become stronger than ever . . . and ultimately emerge the Jeanne Cooper we know today, in whom we are all enormously proud."

Bell's scriptwriters couldn't have penned a better tribute to his leading lady than his heartfelt speech, which concluded, "Dear lady, we salute you on this very, very special day . . . and we love you!"

© BARRY MORGENSTEIN

LINDA DANO

The fabulous Felicia Gallant was one of daytime TV's most flamboyant characters.

Crowning Role: Felicia Gallant on *Another World*

Reign: 1983–99

Other Notable Roles: Cynthia Haines on *As the World Turns* (1981–82) and Gretel Rae Cummings on *One Life to Live* (1978–80; 1999–present)

What Linda Says About Felicia: "Everyone asks, 'Are you like Felicia?' And you know, I don't know what comes first, the chicken or the egg. After fifteen years, you can't not be like your character, I don't think."

Character's Most Notable Pursuit: Finding time to write

Character's Occupations: Romance novelist, talk-show host, businesswoman, bookshop owner, and all around gadabout

Character's Full Name: Felicia Gallant St. George Lindquist Blake Castigliano Radzinsky

Husbands: Louis St. George, Zane Lindquist, Mitch Blake, Lucas Castigliano, and Sergei Radzinsky

Character's Real Name: Fanny Grady

Character's Diva-lution: Felicia Gallant was born on February 23, 1949. Her father died while she was a child, and her mother was remarried to a minister named Noah Grady. Felicia and her stepfather were not close, and when Felicia's mother died, Felicia was left to be raised by an emotionally distant stepparent.

Looking for the affection and love she didn't get at home, Felicia fell in love with Lucas Castigliano, but their affair ended badly when she discovered she was pregnant. Noah told Felicia her baby had died during childbirth, when in fact he had put the baby up for adoption.

In the 1970s, Felicia, now a famous romance novelist, fell in love with a womanizer named Cass Winthrop but ended up marrying Louis St. George instead. After they divorced, Felicia moved to Paris, where she became involved with Carl Hutchins. When it became apparent the relationship was going nowhere, Felicia pulled up stakes and moved to Bay City, where she resumed her affair with Cass. When Felicia discovered that Cass was two-timing her, she broke off their romance. Despite their rocky beginnings, Cass and Felicia managed to remain close friends throughout the years.

Felicia believed she had found her true love when she met Zane Lindquist. Though they seemed like polar opposites, Zane and Felicia complemented one another perfectly. They were married, but later that same year, Zane was killed.

Devastated by Zane's death and convinced she would never find love again, Felicia was surprised to realize she was falling in love with Mitch Blake. She thought she was getting a new lease on life and love when she married Mitch in 1988. But their marriage began to crumble when Mac Cory died, leaving his widow, Rachel—Mitch's true love—free. And when Felicia's first love, Lucas, showed up in Bay City, her marriage to Mitch fell apart completely.

Now reunited, Lucas and Felicia got married and decided to adopt a daughter, Jenna, in part because of the loss of their child so many years earlier. Little did Felicia know, however, that her birth daughter, Lorna, was alive and well and living in Bay City. And as soap irony would have it, Felicia and Lorna were bitter enemies. When she learned the truth about her parentage, Lorna at first resented Felicia and Lucas, but she eventually warmed up to them.

In July 1992, Felicia once again suffered a devastating loss when Lucas was shot and killed. Losing her first love sent Felicia into an emotional tailspin that resulted in her alcoholism. But Felicia couldn't admit she had a problem until she indirectly caused Jenna to have a miscarriage. Felicia had to pull herself together for Lorna's sake in 1993, after the younger woman was raped. To avenge her daughter, Felicia shot the rapist.

In 1995, Felicia was ready to love again and became involved with John Hudson, even though he happened to be married to one of her best friends. Friendship be damned, Felicia accepted John's proposal, but their engagement was called off after she discovered John had slept with his estranged wife.

Helping Felicia get over her broken engagement to John was Alexander Nikos, who bore an uncanny resemblance to Lucas (both characters were played by the same actor, John Aprea). Alexander, however, was way too possessive of Felicia for her tastes and, to top it off, he was somewhat responsible for Felicia falling through a window and severely injuring her face.

Felicia recovered from the fall and afterward looked better than ever. She romanced a much younger man, Sergei Radzinsky. Though Sergei's love for Felicia was real, she thought of him as a friend. She married him to keep him from being deported, and also because she believed he was dying. As the citizens of Bay City called it a day, however, it appeared that the friendship between Felicia and Sergei was beginning to develop into something deeper.

Real-Life Soap Opera: Linda Dano was born May 12 in Long Beach, California. Her early ambition was to be either an interior decorator or fashion designer, but she got into acting after she parlayed a successful modeling career into a three-year contract with 20th Century Fox studios. While under contract she appeared in such films as *Hello, Dolly!, Tony Rome, The Boston Strangler, Wishbone Cutter,* and *Star.*

Linda also made frequent appearances on television, including roles in the television movies *Rage of Angels II, War of the Worlds, Lost Survivor, Perry Mason: The Case of the Killer Kiss,* and *When the Vows Break.* She was a series regular on both *The Fess Parker Show* and *The Montefuscos.*

Since joining *Another World* in 1982, Linda Dano has become one of soapdom's most celebrated stars, but she isn't content to simply act. Entrepreneurial by nature, she has proven herself to be a true "hyphenate." She hosted the Lifetime cable talk show *Attitudes* for six years and became a contributor to New York's local show *Live at Five.* In 1984, she co-authored a Harlequin romance novel, *Dreamweaver,* under the name of her onscreen alter ego, Felicia Gallant. She later authored the books *Looking Great* and *Living Great.* She has also acted as "Fashion File" editor for *Soap Opera Digest,* developed a personal line of fashion accessories for QVC, and is president and CEO of Strictly Personal, a New York–based fashion-consulting service.

"And I'm not just an actress who's decided, *Let me tell you how to do this,*" she adds pointedly. "I do come with credentials."

Dano says that none of her personal accomplishments would be possible without the understanding of her husband, Frank Attardi, a retired advertising executive who has made several appearances on *Another World.*

"You know, the glorious thing about doing a daytime soap is that you don't work every day. I just sort of fill in some of those other time slots with other things. But," she points out, "you can't go out and do all this stuff and then come home at night and have somebody there with a face on who's pissed at you because you've been gone too long. Also, if you have your priorities very clear, I think you can do a lot more than you would think. My priorities are to take care of Frank, be home with the dogs and my mother, make dinner, and because I know that's what I do, I don't spend a lot of time thinking or being distracted by what I do for a living."

When NBC canceled *Another World* in 1999 and most of its cast wondered what their next jobs would be, Dano was quickly snapped up by the ABC network. In a rather unique deal, she signed to reprise her early 1980s *One Life to Live* character, relationship specialist Gretel Rae Cummings, on that show and also make crossover appearances on the other three ABC soaps—*All My Children, General Hospital,* and *Port Charles.*

"ABC called and said, 'What do you think about playing Gretel Cummings and spinning her out over four shows?'" Dano recalled. "I said, 'Are you crazy?' I couldn't even fathom it."

Regardless, she agreed and began work on June 28, 1999, just three days after the *Another World* finale aired. Although she looked forward to her new job, leaving *Another World* was like leaving her family. On the day Linda found out the series was being canceled after thirty-five years (to make way for the new youth-oriented soap *Passions*), Linda says she was so upset she couldn't come in to work.

"I think I was in a state of denial," she says. "Even though I knew for a long time it was coming, it felt like I'd been hit by a car."

But she's also the first to acknowledge that by any standard, thirty-five years is a long time and that new challenges are part of an actor's life.

"Why I act, and why I love to act, is that I love the ride."

Awards and Accolades: Emmy Award for Outstanding Actress for *Another World* (1993).

Most Notable Real-Life Diva Moment: Going public with her facelift. As she entered her early fifties, Dano began to contemplate undergoing cosmetic surgery. More than personal vanity prompted her decision; there were also career factors, such as her awareness that it was taking longer and longer to light her scenes.

"I don't want my audience to be distracted by my jowls," Dano said. "I want them to pay attention to my work. Plus, my age was showing and that's not the character I play."

But there was also a personal reason. "I was once a model, sought after by men. Then I had a double chin, and I don't feel like me."

So right before her fifty-fifth birthday, Linda made the decision to have the procedure. But rather than sneak off for a discreet nip-and-tuck, Dano boldly decided to share the process with her fans. Throughout the entire experience, Dano kept a diary, which was later published in *Ladies Home Journal.* Her facelift was also written into her soap storyline, so that she could recover onscreen, along with her character.

"Felicia is thrown through a skylight, face first, and drops twenty feet and crashes into a table," explained Dano. "The writers wanted her to be so severely damaged that she would need plastic surgery to be recognizable again. That would explain the new me."

Despite all the preparation, it was still nerve-racking. "I was very afraid of the surgery," Dano admits. "I'd never had major surgery before so I didn't know what to expect. And being dramatic, I of course went for the absolute worst: I wouldn't make it, I would die under the anesthetic. I took all of my good luck charms and pictures, but thank God it all worked out. You know, the further away you get from the actual event, the less you remember of the horrors of it."

Linda says that one day on the set after her recovery, she caught sight of herself on a monitor and stopped to stare, saying, "'God, I really look good, don't I?' And everyone on the set cheered. Then we all stopped and had 'a moment.'"

Div-o-Meter: 10—Anyone willing to make a cause célèbre out of their facelift, and who owns both an Emmy and a CEO title, is not to be trifled with.

LESLEY-ANNE DOWN

Down but not out: Sunset Beach was canceled, but TV veteran Lesley-Anne Down always lands on her feet.

Crowning Role: Olivia Richards on *Sunset Beach*

Reign: 1997–99

What Lesley-Anne Says About Olivia: "I don't know what Olivia is. It's really hard for me to stand outside and look in."

Character's Most Notable Pursuit: Keeping one step ahead of her ex-husband

Character's Occupation: Radio broadcast executive

Husband: Gregory Richards (divorced)

Character's Diva-lution: Olivia was married to Gregory Richards for twenty-three years. They had met as youths but Olivia initially avoided Gregory, then a promising law student, because she didn't want him to know she came from a poor family. But eventually, they fell in love and were married.

The couple had a daughter, Caitlin, and they couldn't have been happier. But when Olivia miscarried their next child, a boy, things went downhill. Gregory immersed himself in work and withdrew emotionally from Olivia. Feeling neglected, Olivia turned to other men—and alcohol. Gregory also began having affairs. When Olivia got pregnant with Sean, instead of being happy, Gregory grew more distant out of the fear that he would lose this son as he had his last. So Gregory lavished most of his attention on Caitlin, while Olivia doted on Sean.

Over the years, Olivia and Gregory became near strangers to each other. Once while drunk, Olivia had a fling with Caitlin's old boyfriend, Cole. Terrified that her daughter would find out, Olivia made Cole swear to keep their sexual encounter a secret.

The next family trauma occurred when Sean needed brain surgery. The crisis actually brought Olivia and Gregory closer—but only until Olivia discovered she was pregnant and wasn't sure whether the father was Cole or Gregory. Complicating matters even more, Caitlin was pregnant with Cole's baby. Not knowing Olivia was pregnant, Gregory began plotting to break up Cole and Caitlin so that he and Olivia could raise Caitlin's baby. His scheming didn't work, however, and Olivia didn't get the abortion she had contemplated. After Olivia and Caitlin were in a car accident, Olivia finally told Gregory she was expecting a baby. By then, however, Caitlin had lost hers.

Olivia, however, would not get to raise her own child. The devious Annie Douglas (who wanted to marry Gregory) drugged Olivia and delivered her baby in a remote cabin. Then she immediately turned the baby over to Caitlin, who had not told Cole she had lost their baby. Annie's partner in the baby swap, Dr. Brock, told Olivia that her baby had been stillborn. As if that wasn't enough, Annie also planted the idea in Gregory's head that the baby died because Olivia had been drinking.

Distraught over the perceived death of her child, Olivia tried to commit suicide. Cole, however, saved her life. In an effort to regroup, Olivia left town. When she returned, Annie and Gregory were now a couple. Gregory divorced Olivia and married Annie in Las Vegas. Later, Olivia remembered the truth about the birth of her baby and confronted Annie, who admitted everything.

When the first of two powerful earthquakes struck, Annie saved Olivia's life. She was nearly killed again during the second quake, when Gregory crashed the car they were in. When they got to the hospital, they discovered that Trey, the child Caitlin was raising as her own, needed a medical procedure. Olivia told the doctor that she was actually Trey's mother.

After that revelation, Gregory and Olivia remained at odds, each trying to find ways to bring down the other, succeeding only in bringing down everyone around them.

Real-Life Soap Opera: In 1964, when Lesley-Anne Down was ten, she told her father she wanted to go to work. Thinking he was going to dissuade her, he read her the classified ads to show her there was nothing there for children. To his surprise, however, he found an advertisement that read: "Wanted: Child Models." So began Lesley-Anne's career as a model.

At fourteen, she was called Britain's most beautiful teenager, and a year and a half later she left school to pursue her career full time. When she was sixteen, she left home. Two years later, she came to America to try her luck, and for the next eight years was bi-continental, traveling back and forth between America and London. Over those years, she worked constantly. Among her feature film credits are *Brannigan* with John Wayne and Richard Attenborough, *A Little Night Music* with Elizabeth Taylor, *Rough Cut* with Burt Reynolds and David Niven, and *Hanover Street* with Harrison Ford. She also appeared on *Dallas* and the epic miniseries *North and South.*

During this time she was involved with writer Bruce Robinson (who would later write *The Killing Fields*), a relationship that lasted ten years. She was also married—briefly—to director William Friedkin (*The Exorcist*).

For all her credits, Lesley-Anne's most important role was that of Lady Georgina Wolsey in the classic 1970s British series *Upstairs, Downstairs.* "Getting that series changed my life completely," Down says. In the United States, she starred in the award-winning miniseries *North and South,* which came about only because she had to turn down *The Thorn Birds,* which went instead to Rachel Ward.

"I was pregnant with Jack [whose father is William Friedkin] so I couldn't do it. That changed my life completely because had I done *The Thorn Birds,* I wouldn't have done *North and South,* therefore I wouldn't have met Don and I wouldn't have had my little Georgie."

The Don she refers to is Don FauntLeRoy, whom she met while filming *North and South* and married in 1986. In addition to her sons, Jack and George, Lesley-Anne has two stepdaughters, Juliana and Season, from her marriage to Don.

Like many actresses coming to daytime from the world of features and primetime, Down was amazed at the workload. "As I've said many times, especially to the people who scoff that you're doing a soap opera, I take my hat off and applaud every actor who has ever done them, because they're immensely hard work. You don't realize how mentally demanding they are.

"Not just on a level of learning thirty pages a day, but as a character going through these outrageous plots that they put you in the middle of. Those things do affect you. You are living two lives; you're living your life and the character's life. Some weeks the character's life takes up more hours of your waking moments than your real life does."

Sunset Beach was canceled in 1999, leaving Down free to concentrate on her family and contemplate a day when she might hang up her thespian hat. "I'm truly ready for the gold watch. I'm forty-four and I started work when I was ten—that's thirty-four years I've been working."

Awards and Accolades: She received a Golden Globe nomination for *North and South*.

Most Notable Real-Life Diva Moment: Dumping her first husband to marry director William Friedkin. "I was married to another man in England, who was Argentinean, and I met Billy Friedkin in England," she explains. "And wham, bam, all kinds of things happened in a very brief two-month period, which culminated in me being pregnant and an engagement ring—which was a little prickly because I was already married to the Argentinean.

"But, life being what life is, we sent lawyers off to Cairo who annulled the wedding, and I sort of waddled down Jerry Weintraub's grove, I suppose you'd call it, and the minister pronounced Billy and I man and wife."

Amazingly, she did the same thing a couple of years later.

"I was married to Billy and I was doing *North and South* back in 1984–85," she recalls, "when I met Don. Again, within a couple of months the same routine, I'm really a repetitive person—wham, bam, etc.

"I'm flippant about it and I don't mean to be, because in this instance we both had children. Don had two little girls who were three and five at the time, and I had a little boy [Jack] who was two."

Down and FauntLeRoy have been happily married for thirteen years, and Down believes her impulsive days are over.

Div-o-Meter: 6—She's got the pedigree but she's just too much fun and too straightforward.

The Legend of Sunset Beach

In the 1920s, a Euoropean aristocrat named Armando Deschanel met the woman he believed to be the love of his life—so much so that he agreed to participate in a duel for the right to have her affections. He won but had to flee the country for killing his opponent. Making the situation more tragic was his realization that his paramour didn't love him as he thought she did.

Distraught, Armando traveled to America. As he stood looking out over the Pacific Ocean despairing over lost love and wondering if he would ever find love again, a woman appeared, as if by magic. She came and stood beside him and they fell in love while watching the sunset.

After they married, Armando built a beachfront castle as a monument to their eternal love. Over time, a small beachfront community arose and everyone who lived there was drawn to the area by the hope and romance offered by the tale of Deschanel. The castle is long gone but the legend lives on in the town called Sunset Beach, whose residents believe that when the sun sets, and the Santa Ana winds blow warm and sultry, the first person you see on the far side of the pier is the one you're destined to be with.

MARJ DUSAY

A diva for all seasons: In addition to playing Guiding Light's *wheeling-dealing Alexandra Spaulding, Marj Dusay has also stolen the show on* Capitol, Santa Barbara, *and* All My Children.

Crowning Role: Alexandra Spaulding on *Guiding Light*

Reign: 1993–96; 1998–99

Other Notable Roles: Myrna Clegg on *Capitol* (1983–87); Pamela Capwell Conrad on *Santa Barbara* (1987–88, 1990); and Vanessa Bennett on *All My Children* (1999–present)

What Marj Says About Alex: "I feel great loyalty to Alex, but I couldn't tell what the devil was going to happen to her."

Character's Most Notable Pursuit: Trying to one-up and use her brother before he could one-up and use her

Character's Full Name: Alexandra Spaulding von Halkein Thorpe

Husbands: Baron Leo von Halkein and Roger Thorpe

Character's Diva-lution: Alexandra Spaulding is the daughter of Brandon Spaulding and the owner of a very large company with vaguely explained business dealings. When Alexandra first arrived in Springfield, she was intent on exacting revenge against her brother, Alan, with whom she is fiercely competitive. Alan had ruined her relationship with Eric Luvonaczek, the father of her twin sons— Nick and Lujack. But as often seems to happen in daytime dramas, for some reason, Alex wasn't aware that Nick existed.

Meanwhile, Alex had to contend with the arrival of India von Halkein, her stepdaughter from her failed marriage to a wealthy baron. India was intent on reclaiming the fortune she believed Alex unrightfully took from her father.

Alexandra's darkest hour came when Lujack was killed while rescuing his fiancée from kidnappers. In an effort to pick up the pieces of her life, in 1987 Alexandra became involved with H. B. Lewis, who eventually proposed to her. But after trying to go into business together, the couple broke up. H. B. left town and Alexandra concentrated on work. After failed romances with Hawk Shayne and Fletcher Reade, Alexandra married the villainous Roger Thorpe. Unfortunately, Roger had only married Alex to get his hands on her assets. When she caught him cheating with the much younger Mindy Lewis, Alexandra exacted revenge.

In 1991, Alexandra's other son, Nick McHenry, arrived in Springfield, having followed Mindy Lewis there. Whereas Lujack had been reserved with his affections, once Nick realized that Alexandra was his mother, he embraced her. Now reunited with her son, Alexandra gave him a job at her company and life was good. But Alexandra didn't approve of Nick's relationship with Mindy and tried—but ultimately failed—to prevent the couple from marrying. After that marriage broke up, Susan Bates, who was HIV-positive, left Springfield to be with her.

For a while, after a run in with her sister Amanda, Alexandra also left town. She returned in 1998, concerned that Spaulding Enterprises was not being run properly.

After fading into the background, Alexandra left Springfield once again in 1999.

Of Special Note: Dusay took over the role of Alexandra from the extremely popular **Beverlee McKinsey** (see pages 127–134). Michael Zaslow, who died from Lou Gehrig's disease in 1999, played Alexandra's ex-husband Roger Thorpe.

Real-Life Soap Opera: Marj Dusay was born Marj Mahoney on February 20, 1936, in Russell, Kansas, the second of six children in an Irish/Bohemian family. Although to outsiders, Russell may seem like it's in the middle of nowhere, the Kansas burg actually has a history of producing residents who go on to bigger and better things, including two senators, Bob Dole and Arlen Specter, who attended Marj's alma mater, Russell High School.

After graduating from high school, Marj enrolled at the University of Kansas, but left after her second year to pursue a modeling career in New York. She married and had two children, Randall and Deborah. Marj moved her family to San Francisco where she studied improvisational comedy. But it wasn't until she moved to Los Angeles that her acting career finally took off. Marj joined the groundbreaking improv group The Session, whose members included Richard Dreyfuss and Rob Reiner. She went on to perform in numerous films and more than 150 television episodics, including *The Steve Allen Show, Dallas, In the Heat of the Night, The Fresh Prince of Bel Air, Perfect Strangers, Star Trek, WKRP in Cincinnati,* and *Murder, She Wrote.* She also played the recurring role of Blair's socialite mother on the long-running sitcom, *The Facts of Life.*

Among her most memorable guest spots were her experiences involving *Hawaii Five-0*. "I was asked to read for a part where I would have played a hooker, a very hard, tough woman," Dusay recalls. "So I dressed the part—heavy makeup, ripped hose, the whole bit."

But on her way to the audition, Marj's car broke down. "There I was, in my hooker outfit, out on the L.A. freeway by myself! I thought *I am dead.* They're going to find me dead, and they'll look at me and say, 'Wow, I wonder what she did for a living?'"

Even worse, after she finally got to the audition and read, she didn't get the part. She was, however, cast in another episode that, she recalls, "had some terrible lines, like, 'McGarrett, you got big shoulders. I wanna lean on 'em!' I mean, really. . . . It was corny stuff! Even back then, it was corny. I just told them that, flat-out. I said, 'This sucks! Am I supposed to laugh or cry when I say this?' But I guess they liked what they saw, my reactions or whatever, because I got the part."

Marj made the jump to daytime in 1983 when she assumed the role of Myrna Clegg on the short-lived CBS soap *Capitol*. The role had been originated by Carolyn Jones, who died of cancer in 1983. (Jones was best known to primetime audiences as Morticia on the 1960s comedy *The Addams Family*.)

"Myrna was more into society than politics," Dusay says of her character. "She stuck her pudgy little fingers in there; she was more on the social edge than rather trying to get results politically."

After *Capitol* was yanked from the CBS schedule in 1987 after a five-year run, Marj set sail for *Santa Barbara* to play Pamela Capwell, a role originally slated to be filled by film actress Samantha Eggar.

Dusay finally hit her stride when she was the surprise choice to replace Beverlee McKinsey as *Guiding Light*'s Alexandra Spaulding, making her first appearance in the role on September 24, 1993. Although Marj had her own following, it was a nervous time for the soap's executive producer, Jill Farren Phelps.

"It's virtually impossible to predict what the audience's reaction will be to a character who has become beloved to them. A lot is at stake," she said. "But we know that when Marj walks into a room, everyone will look up and pay attention and that's the quality we need for Alex."

Dusay was not at all intimidated by the circumstances because she had been in those shoes before. "No matter what, you can't do it somebody else's way," she said at the time. "If you try and mimic them it's just a mimic. Carolyn Jones was a great lady and there was no way I could be her. You just have to be you and use the best parts of yourself. If you try to be someone else, it doesn't sell because it's not truthful."

Dusay has a theory on the endurance of daytime dramas. "You know, when you think about it, no wonder the soaps are so popular, because the whole world revolves around family drama—from the president's on down. Let's face it, that's all family drama. You hope what drama does is pinpoint some of the questions you have in your life, and possibly gives you an answer. That's why soaps are so popular. We just want to know how to exist better."

Her high point as Alex came in 1995 when she was nominated for a Daytime Emmy as Outstanding Actress. In a surprising reversal of fortunes, Dusay left *Guiding Light* two years later, according to the official statement, "due to lack of story for the character."

Marj spent little time bemoaning her character's fate and instead turned her attention to the theater, appearing in the play *Good Will* in New York City. Dusay admitted she had "been wanting desperately to do New York theater. It's always been a dream of mine to do theater here, but I never had the time because I've always been busy with TV."

In November 1998, Dusay returned to *Guiding Light* on a non-contract basis for a storyline involving a wedding. A short time later, she was offered a contract to join *All My Children* in a new role, Vanessa Bennett. Bennett is a wealthy widow who just happens to be the mother of the dastardly Dr. David Hayward, played by Vincent Irizarry, who, it also just happens, played Marj's son on *Guiding Light*.

"We didn't tape any last scenes [on *Guiding Light*], because the job came about very quickly. I didn't even know that Vanessa was a full-fledged consummated deal until the last day I was taping at *Guiding Light*. Then *All My Children* wanted an answer, of course, because they wanted to get the part started. Since we didn't have any kind of direction from *Guiding Light* we couldn't afford to play games with the contract being offered. It was kind of one of those things that happened just like that."

If Marj has any regret over leaving *GL,* it's that Alexandra was just allowed to fade away. "I feel badly about it in a way. The last year I was on was such a disappointment; she was just floating with no real intention or action. That's an easy way to lose a character."

Now she finds herself in a completely different situation. "I love the whole set-up—it's brassy, it's showy, it's conniving and loaded with all those wonderful human emotions that have to deal with family and why families don't get along. And it's wonderful to work with Vincent again. It makes me feel so comfortable and calms me down a little bit, because a new role is always a little hysterical-making." She laughs, "I'm fond of hysteria at certain times in my life, though."

Awards and Accolades: Dusay earned a 1995 Daytime Emmy nomination for Outstanding Actress, which pit her against fellow divas Susan Lucci, Leslie Charleson, and Erika Slezak (Slezak won the award).

Causes: Marj served as the Kansas Film Commissioner from 1984 to 1989 and continues to be active in encouraging film production in Kansas.

Most Notable Real-Life Diva Moment: In a true tragedy, her son Randall died in 1993 from AIDS.

Trivia: In 1992, Dusay appeared on *Days of Our Lives* as Vivian Alamain, subbing for Louise Sorel, who was on sick leave due to back problems.

Div-o-Meter: 5—Although quite capable of tearing up the scenery with the best of them, Dusay was never really given the chance to crank up the volume on *Guiding Light*. Her flashier *All My Children* role, however, just may boost her up a few notches.

Capitol

Capitol was the first daytime drama to be introduced during primetime as a special one-hour preview, aired March 26, 1982. It premiered in its regular time slot three days later.

The show's central theme was the power struggle between two feuding political families, the wealthy Cleggs and middle-class McCandlesses, and the star-crossed romance between Julie Clegg and Tyler McCandless. Over the course of the last year, the storylines grew to international proportions, but it wasn't enough to save the soap.

Even though the producers knew their show was going to be canceled, they decided against tying up the storylines. The last episode ended with heroine Sloane Denning facing a firing squad in a fictitious Middle Eastern country. Denning was played by Deborah Mullowney—who is now known as Debrah Farentino, star of the FOX primetime series *Get Real*.

MORGAN FAIRCHILD

From Fatsy Patsy to femme fatale:
Morgan Fairchild.

Crowning Role: Sydney Chase on *The City*

Reign: 1995–96

Other Notable Roles: Jennifer Pace Phillips on *Search for Tomorrow* (1973–77)

What Morgan Says About Sydney: "She's Rupert Murdoch in drag."

Character's Most Notable Pursuit: Mogul-dom

Character's Diva-lution: As Fairchild dryly notes about Chase, the "bright, beautiful, and witty driving force" behind Chase International, a communications mega-conglomerate: "It does get to be, 'Oh, we need a bitch. Let's get Morgan. Or, We need glam. Let's get Morgan.'" Enough said.

Of Special Note: Although Fairchild may not have spent many years as a Daytime Diva, she made up for it in primetime, becoming synonymous with nighttime soap vixen on shows such as *Flamingo Road, Paper Dolls, Falcon Crest,* and *Dallas.*

Real-Life Soap Opera: Although the name Morgan Fairchild suits her perfectly, the actress's real name is Patsy Ann McClenny. She was born February 3, 1950, in Dallas, Texas, the daughter of Martha and Edward McClenny. Morgan readily acknowledges the tremendous impact her mom made not only on her life but also on her career. In the sixth grade, young Patsy was mortified at the idea of having to give an oral report—no doubt partly because as a then-chunky pre-adolescent with a genius level IQ, she was often referred to—believe it or not—as Fatsy Patsy.

"I was fat," admits Morgan. "I had big, thick glasses. I had white eyelashes and white eyebrows and white hair. I was this little pudge who made straight A's and never opened her mouth," which is why, for three days straight she tried—and failed—to give the report. So her mother, a high school English teacher, sent Patsy to an acting class in hopes of helping her overcome her fears. While there, the young girl discovered a natural ability and love for the stage.

And a funny thing happened after she became involved in the theater. The summer prior to her twelfth birthday, according to her sister Cathryn, Morgan was transformed "from a puffy, pasty wallflower to this gorgeous, Marilyn Monroe–like knockout. She discovered makeup, she lost the weight, she blossomed. Everything happened, and when she went back to school the next year, it was like 'wow!'"

Soon after, she began performing in the Highland Park Children's Theatre, and by fourteen she was auditioning for parts at Theatre Three. "I learned so much from them," she says of those early experiences. "When you're young and you're learning, you don't necessarily appreciate the discipline that you're learning. It was community theater but it was community theater that expected a lot of you."

At sixteen, Morgan was hired to be Faye Dunaway's stand-in in *Bonnie and Clyde*. By then, she was acting regularly in theater productions. Her mother encouraged her completely and was there for every rehearsal and stage performance.

After graduating a year early from Lake Highlands High School in Dallas, Morgan attended Southern Methodist University. While in college, she got married. She moved with her new husband to New York in 1971 to pursue her career. The marriage ended in 1973, the same year she was cast in *Search for Tomorrow*.

It was during this time that Patsy felt the need to adopt a new identity and rechristened herself Morgan Fairchild. The name *Morgan* came from the title of the 1966 comedy starring David Warner as an eccentric who's completely misunderstood.

"It was wonderful," Morgan says. "I've always lived in fantasies. That movie saved me when I was a teenager."

Not surprisingly, although her father never completely accepted her new persona, Fairchild's mother embraced it, and to the day she died called her daughter *Morgan*.

On *Search for Tomorrow*, Fairchild played Jennifer Phillips, a murderer and all-around villain. Morgan was so good in the part that she found herself being typecast. The actress initially resisted being pegged as a bad girl, until a director gave her a friendly piece of advice during the filming of the 1978 telefilm *The Initiation of Sarah*.

"He said, 'Honey, I can get an ingenue anywhere. But a good bitch is hard to find.'" It was a comment Fairchild would never forget and would later use to her advantage.

During the 1980s, after moving to Los Angeles, Morgan Fairchild became a staple of primetime soapdom in roles such as Constance

Carlyle on *Flamingo Road,* Jordan Roberts on *Falcon Crest,* and Racine
on *Paper Dolls.* Through it all, Fairchild was able to keep perspective.

"People have a preconceived notion about what people in Hollywood are like," she notes. "And I have several things going against
me. I live in Hollywood, I'm an actress, I'm a woman, and I'm
blonde. I mean, you've got all the strikes against you. And so, literally, if I can walk and chew gum at the same time, they think it's
really neat.

"For most of my life, because of what I look like, I've been conscious of an image," she continues. "They think I'm the cheerleader
or the homecoming queen; that I'm prim, proper, elegant, porce-
lain. So I played a series of what I call elegant vixens, and people
begin to see you that way. They perceive you as something you're
not. So, anything I can do to send that up to bring it back to reality is
something I enjoy." Which is why Morgan has never passed up an
opportunity to give herself a public tweak. "I've always loved pok-
ing fun at that glamorous public image of me," she says. "I like to take
the blonde icon thing and twist it all over the place," such as when
her soap diva character on the sitcom *Cybill* was hurled off a cliff.
"I wish," she says, "someone would do a sitcom where I spoofed
myself." She has also exercised her comedy muscles on *Friends* (as
Matthew Perry's mother) and *Roseanne* (as Sandra Bernhard's girlfriend).

Typecasting or no, Fairchild has worked consistently over the
course of her career and is an instantly recognizable face and name,
which is why ABC came a-calling when they were desperate to
jumpstart *The City,* the relaunched version of the failed soap *Loving.*

"We wanted a primetime diva to get attention for the new show,"
said Pat Fili-Krushel, head of ABC's Daytime division. "Morgan was
my ideal. When you hear Morgan Fairchild, you know what you're
getting. She is a business."

Although primetime's reigning diva had no intention of returning to daytime, she relented after ABC threw a TV movie, a series pilot, and a reported $1 million salary in as incentive—all in exchange for a one-year commitment. Even so, it was personally difficult. Besides the sixteen-hour days, it meant being separated from her longtime life partner, film executive Mark Seiler.

Another downside, Fairchild once said, was the pressure of maintaining her soap opera wardrobe.

"I'm so sick of clothes I could die. I'm sick of the work that goes into the clothes and the look and the image. But this is how I know it matters: I was at the gym last week, and two guys came up to me—separately, mind you—and told me they loved the red suit I was wearing in the title shots for *The City*. And they were both straight!

"This tells me the work it takes to put it all together is worth the effort. . . . They're not paying me to play a charwoman. They're paying me to show up looking glam and, damn it, I'm gonna show up looking glam!"

The irony is that Fairchild wore mostly her own clothes while on the soap.

Since leaving *The City,* Morgan has kept busy in film and television. "I just keep plugging away," Morgan says. "That in itself is an accomplishment. There aren't that many parts for women these days, particularly if you're over twenty-five." Ah, but a good bitch is timeless.

Awards and Accolades: Fairchild has been twice nominated for primetime Emmys.

Causes: Fairchild is dedicated to a number of issues, including pro-choice, AIDS, global warming, deforestation, and overpopulation.

She was a member of the Family AIDS Network board of directors, founded by Mary Fisher in 1992 to "provide programmatic leadership in education, prevention, diagnosis, and treatment, especially for women and people of color, the populations now most at risk for becoming HIV-infected."

Trivia: After Fairchild opted not to extend her contract for *The City,* she was replaced as the show's headliner by Emmy-winning soap superstar Jane Elliot, whose villainous character, Tracy Quartermaine, was transplanted from *General Hospital.* Elliot had been playing the role on and off since 1978. The decision was made to have Tracy acquire a major interest in the building where Sydney Chase lived—on the day Sydney moved out.

"It was all the network's idea," says Elliot. "Morgan was leaving and it was a very big loss for the show. It was already in the works that I was returning to *General Hospital* for a while so the move was one of those bright ideas, like a lightbulb going on in someone's head."

Div-o-Meter: 4—Despite the glam and bitchy stereotype, Morgan is too self-aware and self-mocking to be a serious diva.

SUSAN FLANNERY

*Double-duty diva: Susan Flannery,
the first woman to simultaneously
direct and act in a daytime drama.*

Crowning Role: Stephanie Forrester on *The Bold and the Beautiful*

Reign: 1987–present

Other Notable Roles: Laura Horton on *Days of Our Lives* (1966–75)

Character's Most Notable Pursuit: Running others' lives

Character's Occupation: Businesswoman and professional matriarch

Husband: Eric Forrester

Character's Diva-lution: Stephanie Forrester is the quintessential clan matriarch whose primary goal in life is to keep her family together and make sure they—and everyone else—do what she thinks they ought to do.

That philosophy hasn't always endeared Stephanie to those closest to her and has made her more than a few enemies. One of her
fiercest rivals was Sheila Carter, who poisoned Stephanie by putting
minute traces of mercury in her food, causing Steph to act as though
she were having a mental breakdown. The truth was finally discovered when Stephanie checked herself into the hospital.

A major source of familial conflict has been Stephanie's determination to make sure her beloved sons, Ridge and Thorne, stay away
from Brooke Logan. Stephanie's manipulations eventually drove off
her husband, Eric—sending him straight into the arms of her
enemy, Brooke Logan. Although Stephanie is the rarest of divas—the
one-man kind—she did have a fling with Jack Hamilton after her
divorce, but she still truly only has eyes for Eric, whom she finally
remarried in 1999.

Stephanie once suffered an emotional breakdown that resulted
in amnesia and led to her living on the street as a homeless person.
During that time, she befriended another homeless woman, Ruth.
When Stephanie regained her memory, she made sure Ruth was
reunited with her own family, evidence that Stephanie does deep
down care about people—she just has a weird way of showing it
at times.

Real-Life Soap Opera: A native New Yorker, Susan Flannery took
her educational show on the road west, earning her undergraduate
degree at Stephens College in Missouri before moving on to Arizona
State University to pursue her graduate work in theater arts.

Unlike other hopefuls arriving in Hollywood, Susan never really
had to play the struggling actress role. She was discovered early on
by noted producer Irwin Allen, who cast her in the television series
Voyage to the Bottom of the Sea. Not long afterward, she won the role
of Dr. Laura Horton on *Days of Our Lives.* She stayed on the soap for

eight years and earned an Outstanding Actress Emmy during her tenure. The role is currently being played by another diva, **Jaime Lyn Bauer** (see pages 17–23).

She followed that with a Golden Globe Award for her motion picture debut, *The Towering Inferno,* in which she played Robert Wagner's doomed lover.

Throughout her daytime career, Flannery has successfully ventured into primetime in projects such as Arthur Hailey's miniseries *The Moneychangers,* the TV movies *Anatomy of a Seduction* and *Women in White,* and the series *Dallas.*

Flannery has also established herself as a force behind the camera as a director, earning a Director's Guild Award nomination for helming *The Bold and the Beautiful.* She was the first woman to simultaneously direct and act in a daytime drama.

"The rate you have to work at as a director is sheer insanity," Flannery says. "But directing soaps is fun because you have to think it out. It's not like movies—here you're out there doing the whole job yourself."

When directing, Flannery draws on her personal experience. "The most effective soap scenes to me are what I call 'coffee cup' scenes: two people just talking. What the soap audience wants is a sense of intimate reality. A lot of [soap] directors are afraid of the emotional content, so they move their actors all over the set. The answer to good storytelling is not physical movement; it's plot action."

Flannery is exacting with her castmates because she feels a responsibility to teach the younger actors to be professionals. "I've always been very serious with other actors. If they don't work hard, then I just refuse to work with them."

The multi-dimensional actress is also a licensed pilot, a gourmet cook, and producer of the cable soap *New Day in Eden.*

Awards and Accolades: Flannery won a Daytime Emmy as Outstanding Actress for *Days of Our Lives,* and received a Director's Guild Award nomination as Outstanding Director in a Daytime Drama for *The Bold and the Beautiful.* She also received a Golden Globe Award for Best Movie Debut for the 1974 film *Towering Inferno.*

Div-o-Meter: 10—for being an equally commanding force in front of and behind the camera.

EILEEN FULTON

Eileen Fulton plays the much-married Lisa,
daytime's first superstar bad girl.

Crowning Role: Lisa Grimaldi on *As the World Turns*

Reign: 1960–1964, 1965, 1967–1983, 1984–present

Character's Most Notable Pursuit: Social climbing

What Eileen Says About Lisa: "Years ago I don't think I would have enjoyed having her in my house. When I was first on the show, I liked playing the lying, scheming, conniving person that Lisa was then; she was devoid of any kind of joy. Now, Lisa's a nice person. A little dippy, but nice."

Character's Full Name: Lisa Miller Hughes Eldridge Shea Colman McColl Mitchell Grimaldi. She had one marriage, to Martin Chedwyn, annulled. Marrying Lisa could be dangerous. Four of her husbands—Michael Shea, Whit McColl, Earl Mitchell, and Eduardo Grimaldi—were murdered.

Character's Diva-lution: On May 18, 1960, Eileen Fulton originated the character of Lisa Miller—eventually turning her into the
first superstar bad girl of daytime, which, as it turned out, was not
exactly what the producers originally had in mind.

"Because we were live," explains Fulton, "once you got on the
air, you could really do what you thought was right and they couldn't
do anything about it, because once it was done, it was out of their
hands. That is exactly what I did with Lisa, because she was supposed
to be a sweet girl, and I thought, I am damn tired of playing the
sweet girl next door. I came to New York to be an actor and create
new lives, not to be who I am.

"So I waited until air time and on air I just thought my thoughts,
my devious and conniving thoughts and it just shot right across to
the audience and to Irna Phillips," she recalls, referring to the soap's
co-creator. "Irna said, 'That little rascal can play a bitch!' And so she
started to write for me instead of firing me."

According to the character's back-story, Lisa was an only child
who grew up in Rockford, Illinois, the heir to a local newspaper
empire. Once in Oakdale, *As the World Turns*'s fictional setting, Lisa
wasted no time wreaking havoc.

"Lisa was a real live scheming conniving person," laughs Fulton
of her early years on the soap. "It was a wonderful character part.
This is why I'm an actor. . . . I want to live different lives."

Lisa's first marriage was to Bob Hughes, her college sweetheart. Their son, Tom, was born soon after. But being a stay-at-home
mom while her young doctor husband spent long hours at the hospital was not Lisa's idea of marital bliss. After having a brazen affair
with shoe salesman Bruce Elliott, she divorced Bob and moved to
Chicago, where she married John Eldridge, had an affair with his
brother, and bore another son, Scott. But her conniving caught up
with her. Lisa ended up returning to Oakdale and leaving Scott in

Chicago to be raised by Eldridge, who didn't believe he was the child's real father.

Lisa then became pregnant by scheming doctor Michael Shea and gave birth to another son, Chuckie. Lisa desperately wanted to marry Shea, but he'd have nothing to do with her. As Chuckie got older, Michael changed his mind, but by this time Lisa wanted nothing to do with him. "This is what Irna Phillips did so well," notes Fulton. "She'd get people almost together and then one person didn't want the other, and on and on." Michael resorted to blackmailing Lisa into marriage, but in a bit of poetic justice, he was murdered soon after they wed.

Lisa spent little time grieving. She soon wed Grant Colman, in one of Fulton's favorite storylines. "It was about two people who really loved each other, and for the first time in Lisa's many love affairs—and she'd had affairs with practically everybody—she was being careful. When she fell in love with Grant Colman, she decided for once that she was going to do it right and she wouldn't go to bed with him until after they were married, so that was fun."

But their marriage couldn't overcome the strain caused by Grant's vengeful ex-wife, Joyce, and they eventually divorced, although Grant and Lisa remained close friends. Tycoon Whit McColl was Lisa's next husband, but their union was short-lived. Like Michael Shea, Whit was also murdered.

Perhaps realizing she should lay off marriage a while, Lisa opened a fashion boutique before finding herself once again falling in love, this time with an undercover Interpol agent, Earl Mitchell. And once again, death came a-calling when Earl was murdered tracking down a suspect.

As often happens in the magical world of soaps, children often grow up quickly—at times, literally overnight. "It's one of those funny things that happens on daytime live," Fulton says, recalling earlier days when, "on a Friday afternoon, I had to walk in and give Chuckie a little glass of orange juice and I said, 'Well Chuckie, I hope you have a good day at kindergarten.' And on Monday I said, 'Have a good day at college.'" (Chuckie died in a car accident in the 1970s.)

In the 1990s, Lisa tried to establish ties with Scott, the son she left in Chicago in the 1960s. The grown-up Scott moved to Oakdale and managed to romance Lisa's rival Lucinda Walsh and both of Lucinda's half-sisters, Neal Alcott and Samantha Markham. After failing to rekindle his relationship with Samantha, Scott left town.

In 1995, Lisa married a dashing and mysterious Maltese businessman, Eduardo Grimaldi, whose business dealings were quite possibly corrupt. Not that it mattered. Eduardo, played by Nicolas Coster (who also portrayed Lisa's second husband, John Eldridge), soon met a violent death at the hands of Orlena Grimaldi, his cousin by marriage. But Lisa wrongly believed Eduardo had died because Dr. John Dixon hadn't treated him quickly enough. Lisa pressed charges and almost ruined John's career before he was exonerated. Vowing revenge, John pretended to be in love with Lisa, only to humiliate her at their engagement party.

Lisa's unlucky-in-love streak continued with Martin Chedwyn, who she discovered was using her to launder his assets out of Hong Kong. Martin held Lisa hostage on a yacht and forced her to marry him. Eventually Lisa was rescued by John Dixon, Martin was arrested, and the marriage was annulled.

Fulton admits she was relieved when that particular storyline had completed its arc. "I despised with a passion the whole cartel/Hong Kong storyline. It was totally not Lisa, it was not soap opera, it was devastating. I tried to do the best I could. I couldn't say, 'I'm not going to do it!' because the storyline was already plotted. We tried to make it better, and I think that Simon Prebble, who played Martin Chedwyn, was wonderful. He did the best he could with it."

Over the years, as she bounced back from each tragedy, Lisa's conniving side has mellowed a bit, although her search for love has not. Most recently, she had another go-round with John Dixon, although this time, their attraction to one another was genuine. John's lingering feelings for his ex-wife Barbara—and the interference of the manipulative Carly Tenney—prevented the couple from finding happiness.

Eileen, for one, hopes that Lisa gets another chance to find romance. "Oh, I hope so. She needs to have another husband. She's a romantic. She needs to fall in love," Fulton says, before adding dryly, "Lisa is not like Eileen."

Of Special Note: From May to September 1965, Fulton starred as Lisa Miller Hughes in the *As the World Turns* primetime spin-off *Our Private World,* which had Lisa moving from Oakdale to Chicago. CBS hoped the series would be able to compete with *Peyton Place.* It couldn't. Once the spin-off was canceled, Lisa moved back to Oakdale. *Our Private World* was the first—and to date, only—primetime series spun off from a daytime drama.

Real-Life Soap Opera: Eileen Fulton was born Margaret Elizabeth McLarty on September 13, 1933, in Asheville, North Carolina. As a child she showed a flair for the dramatic and used writing as her creative outlet after receiving a special gift from her father, a Methodist minister. "It's a hardbound book and the cover says, *Showboat* by Edna Ferber," explains Fulton. "But it isn't a real copy of *Showboat.* The pages on the inside are all blank, because it was used as a dummy to put in the bookstore window. Daddy gave me that blank book and said, 'Here, old girl, write a book!' And I did! I was in the third grade, and I wrote all kinds of little short stories. The stories would just come so fast in my mind and things would happen to these characters so quickly, that I didn't have the ability to keep up sometimes in the writing, so I'd draw a picture. It's my favorite memento."

Fulton studied music and drama at Greensboro College in North Carolina, making her professional debut in *The Lost Colony,* an annual drama presentation in Manteo, North Carolina. In 1956, she moved to New York City and studied acting at the Neighborhood Playhouse School of the Theater, planning for a career on the stage. Even after being cast on *As the World Turns,* Eileen would keep in touch with her theater roots. At one point, Fulton worked mornings on the soap, afternoons in matinee presentations of *Who's Afraid of Virginia Woolf?* on Broadway, and evenings in the Off-Broadway musical *The Fantastiks.*

"Friday nights I did *The Fantasticks* at the Sullivan Theater, then a Saturday matinee of *Who's Afraid of Virginia Woolf?* followed by an early show and a late show at the Sullivan, then a Sunday matinee and Sunday evening, and Monday morning they made sure I was back at 7:30 on the dot," she said of the almost superhuman workload. "And back then, we were a half-hour, three- or four-people show, and we did many, many scenes. There was a lot of dialogue, much more than we have today, and it was all live—which was scary," she said.

Perhaps not as frightening as the awesome and unique power of television to touch people's lives, of which she first became aware shortly after she joined the soap. "Lisa had just married Bob. I was being awful. I was just running around with Bruce in the bushes and all of that stuff."

Fulton was standing in front of Saks Fifth Avenue when a woman, fashionably dressed in a pink Chanel suit, approached her and asked if she were Lisa. "And I thought, *Oh, my first autograph!* I said, 'Why, yes that's the part I play!'"

Fulton reached into her purse to grab a pen but stopped abruptly when the woman hissed, "Oh, I hate you!"

"Then she bopped me right there; knocked me across the street, knocked my pen in the gutter. Everybody stood and looked at me like, *Oh you horrible sneaky little devil!* And they let that woman just walk away!"

Run-ins with fans were the least of Fulton's concerns. It was during this time that Fulton quit the soap for the first time, not due to her hectic schedule, but because of the changes she saw happening to her character. "Lisa had been such a sneak and a devil and was such fun, and then she suddenly had to be so full of remorse and feel so sorry for herself. I hated slopping around and feeling sorry for myself, and it got to be a bore. My plate was full so I decided to leave. Just willy-nilly like that."

After a short time away, however, Fulton felt the soap's siren song and returned, only to be hit by wanderlust two other times. "The last time I quit forever in 1983, I went all over the country to do different plays and dinner theaters." Fulton has been back on the show since 1984, but says she is sometimes "annoyed when the writers don't see the importance of me."

Fulton appeared in the Off-Broadway productions of *Abe Lincoln in Illinois, Many Loves, Summer of the Seventeenth Doll,* and *Nite Club Confidential.* She has also appeared in regional theater productions such as *Plaza Suite, It Had to Be You, The Owl and the Pussycat, Cat on a Hot Tin Roof,* and *Goodbye, Charlie.* Her lone film credit was a supporting role in *Girl of the Night.*

Although Fulton became famous as an onscreen bad girl, there was a time when she was earning the same reputation offcamera due to her staunch refusal to play a grandmother. It's a saga worth a soap opera storyline of its own.

"I had a lot of trouble with producers over the years telling me that if I didn't consent to becoming a grandmother, they were going to kill Lisa," explains Eileen. "It was when I asked for a ridiculous amount of time off to do other things. Because back in the 1970s, Lisa was having this hot affair with Michael Shea and they grew Tom up. I went away on vacation and came back and he was going to get married to Carol. And I said, 'He cannot get married because if he gets married that means that I will be a grandmother. They said, 'Well yes, of course, a legitimate grandmother.'

"I was in my thirties and too young to be a grandmother. Grandmothers at that time in the seventies, they took away their love life, they took away the bedroom, they took away everything. Stuck them in the kitchen and that was the end of them. Because they didn't realize that grandparents and older people have a jolly good life, let me put it that way."

When Fulton balked, the producers tried to play hardball. "They told me if I was going to hold them up, they would just simply kill Lisa."

Not one to be cowed, Fulton called their bluff. "I just said, 'I will not be a grandmother. I am too young. It is absurd and I will not do it.'"

"At that time Pat Bruder [Ellen Stewart] was playing a grandmother, and she is younger than I am. She had to wear her hair up in a little bun, and she made it a character part. Barbara Berjer [Claire Lowell] is just a young woman. And what did they do? They couldn't handle it so they hit her with a truck! And I said, 'No, this is not going to happen to me!'"

Fulton refused to re-sign her contract "unless I had a 'grandma clause.' They said, 'What do you mean?' I said, 'My contract is up. I will not re-sign; do whatever you like. I will not re-sign if you make me a grandmother.' So they had to put it in, because I was serious and I had horrible fights about this. In fact I almost broke my hand slamming it on a desk, but anyway, I got that clause and for many years Tom was not, could not, be a father."

Fulton readily admits that she was pushing producers to the limits, but points out she couldn't have done it without clout. "It was so important to me, to have a say in Lisa and to keep her going. If it were not for the grandma clause, I don't even know if Lisa would be on the show now." Fulton eventually relented, and her character has since become a grandmother, but for a time, the infamous grandma clause caused quite a stir among *As the World Turns* fans. She relates, "When Tom and Margo lost their baby, the audience remembered the clause, which I had long since forgotten about, and blamed me. . . . They blamed me, Eileen Fulton, for the death of this pillow! And I got life threatened. Oh, terrible letters."

It's ironic that Susan Lucci made a career out of her eighteen-year Emmy drought considering Fulton has only been nominated for an Emmy once in her illustrious career. Even more amazing is the fact that she hasn't even been asked to be a presenter. True to her style, Fulton's response was to ignore the Emmy's right back, attending the ceremony only once in her first twenty-six years on television.

"You have to pay $250," she was once quoted as saying, "so I threw the invitations away."

She also decided to have a little fun at the Academy's expense. "All the actors get to choose the category they'd like to be in, and I wasn't going to put myself down for anything," says Eileen, "but I was told I had to choose something, and that's when I got smart. I thought I was never going to win anyway, so I chose Aging Ingenue, which of course isn't a real category." Fulton eventually settled on submitting herself in the Supporting category, which resulted in her first, and only, nomination, in 1988.

Although some actors have spent their careers bemoaning their perceived lack of recognition, Fulton doesn't believe in wasting time fretting over what might have been. In an age when day players have delusions of grandeur, Fulton remains pragmatic. When asked if she ever dreamed of feature film stardom, Eileen quickly acknowledges, "Of course I did. But I was never at the right place at the right time. Yet when I look at it, I think I am so lucky to have all these years on this show. It's just wonderful, because I do have a good contract and I can go out and do some other things."

One of those "other things" is singing. Over the last decade or so, Fulton has earned a reputation as a classy, talented cabaret singer, and she has performed in nightclubs and one-woman shows around the country. "I love cabaret. It gives me a chance to play several different characters in one evening."

Another thing she does is write. In addition to her two biographies, *How My World Turns* and *As My World Still Turns,* she has written six murder mysteries: *Take One for Murder; Death of a Golden Girl; Dying for Stardom; Lights, Camera, Death; A Setting for Murder;* and *Fatal Flashback.*

Somehow, she also managed to develop a line of costume jewelry that she tirelessly promotes on the Home Shopping Network. "That's the way Eileen likes it," she laughs. "I like to keep busy."

Curiously, despite all her personal success and having been a star in her own right for several decades, Fulton can still be surprisingly down to earth, such as when she had the opportunity to meet a longtime stage idol. "About ten years ago, I went after getting an autograph from Helen Hayes. We were both doing a charity function at the United Nations for UNICEF, and it was a big banquet. I felt funny going up and asking her for her autograph, so a friend at my table went up to her and said, 'Would you do this autograph for Miss Fulton? She is sitting right over there.'

"Helen looked up and waved to me, and I waved back. She wrote, *Dear Lisa—Love, Helen Hayes.* Isn't that wonderful? That was definitely one of my finer autographs."

As it turns out, Fulton is wonderfully honest about being a fan in her own right. "I've also had my picture taken with Tom Jones. I love him. I think he is spectacular. And Tony Bennett—I don't just want that man's autograph! I have had dinner with him. I have sat and talked with him. I have gone to his concerts. I have had my picture taken with him. I admit it: I would beg, borrow, or steal to get Tony Bennett's autograph!"

Unlike some performers who, having spent the majority of their lives in the public eye and under scrutiny from the media, tend to become bitter toward the press, Fulton maintains a refreshing equanimity about being a celebrity.

"To be honest, I've been very fortunate over the years. I really haven't had a bad experience with the press. Actually, reporters are really not all that bad," she says, but notes, "If you kick them away, they are going to say what they want to say, and what they think the public wants to read. They will say whatever makes good copy. But if you simply talk to them, they will have to say what you said."

That same common-sense approach also guides Fulton as she plans for her future in the *As the World Turns* universe. "As long as I have something fun to do and I'm not bored, I'll be there."

Awards and Accolades: Though she doesn't have an Emmy, Fulton's mantel has no shortage of awards. She was named Best Actress in 1970 by *Daytime TV Magazine*'s readers poll and remained in the top ten in this category for fifty-eight of the first eighty issues, which were printed between 1970 and 1977. She won the title of Best Loved Bad Girl in 1973, and in 1976 she was presented an award for Favorite Female Serial Actress on *The Dinah Shore Show.* In 1991, Fulton received *Soap Opera Digest*'s Editor's Award, and in 1996, she was nominated for a Soap Opera Award from *Soap Opera Digest*.

On September 14, 1998, Fulton was inducted into the Soap Opera Hall of Fame along with *All My Children*'s Ruth Warrick; *General Hospital*'s fabled producer, Gloria Monty; and *Guiding Light*'s casting director, Betty Rea, who cast future Hollywood notables such as Kevin Bacon, Meg Ryan, and Marisa Tomei.

Causes: Fulton has been an active supporter of such charities as UNICEF, the March of Dimes, Cerebral Palsy, the Lupus Foundation, and Martha's Table, an organization in Washington, D.C., that benefits poor and homeless mothers and children. An unabashed advocate for women's rights, Eileen has also devoted herself to numerous causes committed to the betterment of women in society.

In addition, she has established a music scholarship in her late father's name at Brevard College in North Carolina and a Fine Arts scholarship in her own name and her mother's at their alma mater, Greensboro College.

Feuds: Although speculation has been rife that a feud has developed between Fulton and Elizabeth Hubbard, who plays Lucinda, Eileen dismisses the rumor as completely untrue.

"Absolutely not! I think Elizabeth Hubbard is a marvelous person. She's a very smart woman and I admire her very much. No, there is no animosity with anyone. I hate to sound like a goody two-shoes, I really do, but when other people have come on our show from other shows, they say, 'What a wonderful group of people! Everyone is so kind.' And I think, *Aren't people kind on other shows?* It always stymies me when I hear that."

Most Notable Real-Life Diva Moment: Fulton divorced her third husband, landscape architect Rick McMorrow, in 1990, after just three months of marriage. "I had to go to divorce court just like they do on soaps," said Fulton at the time. "A judge came out in a long robe, a bailiff shouted, 'Order, order,' and I took the stand wearing my black divorce suit with a diamond pin just like they do on soap operas. I tell you, life is getting more like a soap every day."

Unlike her soap character, Fulton says she's had enough of matrimony. "It's best to be Eileen Fulton, with her three husbands, instead of Lisa Miller with her seven. If I get committed to one person, I think I'm going to have to be committed to some institution."

Historical Footnote: Eileen Fulton, Helen Wagner, and Don Hastings (Lisa, Nancy, and Bob) were in the November 22, 1963, episode that was interrupted by Walter Cronkite's announcement of the assassination of President John F. Kennedy.

Trivia: Jane Powell filled in as Lisa Grimaldi after Fulton underwent an emergency appendectomy in 1996.

Pamela King (1964) and Betsy von Furstenberg (1983–84) portrayed Lisa during Fulton's extended leaves of absence.

As the World Turns expanded to an hour-long show on December 1, 1975.

Div-o-Meter: 8—Her longevity and fight for the grandma clause is offset by her lack of pretentiousness, as reflected by her shyness in asking stage doyen Helen Hayes for an autograph.

Divas in Training

SOME OF TODAY'S STARS WHO ARE POISED FOR DIVADOM

It's hard to predict who will mature into the divas of tomorrow, especially as the environment within soap operas is constantly changing. Probably gone forever are the days when a soap can debut and remain on the air for three decades, giving audience members and actors the chance to literally grow up with one another. The following are a few actresses who may one day take the reins—and reigns—over from today's Luccis and Halls.

Cady McClain (Dixie Martin, *All My Children*)—Dixie's long-suffering love life and humble beginnings belie a strength of character that has translated into longevity. One of the keys to being a diva is outlasting the others.

Debbi Morgan (Dr. Ellen Burgess, *Port Charles*)—Her medical know-how combined with her no-nonsense attitude gives her a diva quality dignity.

Kelly Ripa (Hayley Vaughan, *All My Children*)—Once a tough-as-nails bad girl, Hayley is maturing into a young woman not to be taken lightly.

Maura West (Carly Tenney, *As the World Turns*)—Like any good diva, Carly wants it all—love, money, and success—and will stop at nothing to get it.

Liza Huber (Gwen Hotchkiss, *Passions*)—What can we say? When your mom is Susan Lucci, it's inevitable.

Soap opera icon Deidre Hall.

DEIDRE HALL

Crowning Role: Dr. Marlena Evans on *Days of Our Lives*

Reign: 1976–87, 1991–present

What Hall Says About Marlena: "When I began playing her back in the late '70s, Marlena was driven, determined, focused, and human. In the '70s that was a thing we were all reaching for, *Now, I can actually have a career!* She was doing it so she became a role model.

"In the '80s, she fell in love, had her family, had tragedy, had success, had joy. Marlena was flawed. She couldn't cook. She wasn't organized. But she was devoted, loyal, driven, and wildly compassionate. I think she was who we all wanted to be, at some point."

Character's Full Name: Dr. Marlena Evans Craig Brady Black

Character's Husbands: Don Craig, Roman Brady, and John Black

Character's Diva-lution: Within a very short time of being introduced, Marlena Evans became one of the most popular characters in
daytime. Not to mention one of the most unlucky. Whereas some
soap characters are doomed to float from one failed relationship to
another, the always-elegant Marlena became a magnet for strange
and unusual happenings. If she wasn't being kidnapped by a gangster,
held captive by the Salem Strangler, or unjustly confined to a psychiatric ward, she found herself possessed by the devil and floating all
over the room à la Linda Blair in *The Exorcist.*

Through it all, however, she remained neatly coifed with near-
perfect makeup. This is not to say that Marlena hasn't had traumas of
the heart, but even her romantic entanglements haven't been com-
monplace. Case in point: the strange saga of the two Romans. The
first Roman was played by Wayne Northrop. After Northrop left the
show, Drake Hogestyn was brought in as the new Roman, said to
have undergone extensive plastic surgery. A few years later, Northrop
returned to the show as Roman, which left Marlena in a quandary—
just who was the man she believed was her husband? In therapy,
Marlena uncovered his true identity: the mysterious John Black.

While helping John Black with his quest to find out about his
past, Marlena was torn between her feelings for Roman and John.
Through it all, she was perpetually tormented by the evil Stefano
DiMera, who wanted to possess her himself. Finally, in 1999,
Marlena married John, but their problems are far from over.

Real-Life Soap Opera: Deidre Hall was born in Milwaukee,
Wisconsin, minutes after her twin sister, Andrea. Soon afterward,
their parents, John and Jean Hall, moved the family to Lake Worth,
Florida, which Deidre describes as being "a cozy, comfortable, safe
town where nothing rippled the water."

Even as a child, Hall displayed the determined ambition that would become one of her most identifiable traits. When she was twelve, Deidre decided she wanted to win the title of Junior Orange Bowl Queen, despite the fact that her parents couldn't afford to send their daughter to modeling classes. Undeterred by her lack of funding, Hall learned the fundamentals of modeling from a friend and proceeded to walk away with the contest title.

"The odd thing," Deidre would say later, "was that I wasn't the prettiest girl by any stretch. But there's a prettiness that has nothing to do with prettiness. It's about confidence."

Hall enrolled at a local junior college but there was never a question in her mind that her destiny lay elsewhere. Once out of school, she moved to Los Angeles and quickly found work modeling and acting. One of her first roles was playing nurse Barbara Anderson on *The Young and the Restless,* from 1973 to 1975. Her first starring role was a far cry from the dramatic emoting of daytime. Hall got her first major break on the Saturday morning children's show *ElectraWoman and DynaGirl* (1976–77), playing a reporter who also fought crime in the guise of superhero ElectraWoman.

From there, she was cast as Marlena in *Days of Our Lives* and over the next eleven years became a soap opera icon. But Hall wasn't content to merely be one of the queens of daytime. She was one of the first soap stars to make a go of it in primetime when she starred in the NBC drama *Our House,* playing a single mom raising three kids (including future *90210* star Shannen Doherty) with the help of her father-in-law, played by Wilford Brimley.

From 1986 to 1987, Hall did double duty, maintaining her role on *Days* while also working on *Our House.* But after the nighttime series was picked up for a second season, Hall left the soap. Marlena was seemingly killed off, much to the dismay of her legion of fans.

Deidre understood how her audience felt but said, "Doing both shows was an enormous undertaking."

But in its second season, *Our House* suffered from falling ratings and rising tension between Brimley and Hall. To her bitter disappointment, the series was canceled, leaving Hall without a job for the first time in more than a decade.

Despite the professional setback, Hall's personal life was going well again and Deidre found herself in a new romantic relationship. As successful as she was professionally, her love life had been much bumpier. In 1970, prior to moving to California, Hall had married a would-be singer-songwriter named Keith Barbour. "We did a lot of growing up together," Deidre says. Like many couples who marry too young, however, Deidre and Keith outgrew each other and they finally divorced in 1977, although they remained close friends.

For the next many years, Hall concentrated on her career, until she fell in love with television executive Michael Dubelko, who at the time was working for *uber*-producer Stephen J. Cannell. The couple first met in 1986 and were married a year later in October 1987. Her happiness, however, would be short-lived; in October 1989, almost two years to the day after they were married, Hall filed for divorce. Friends cited Deidre's career as the reason for the split, with Dubelko wanting more of a stay-at-home wife than Hall was willing to be.

"It wasn't a bad divorce," she says. "In fact, we're still great friends. It's just hard to admit that you've failed."

As far as Deidre is concerned, there's no reason not to remain friends with her exes. "Keith didn't become a bad guy and Michael is a dream. We had a lot of adjusting to do when the marriages didn't work, but rather than yank each other to pieces, we helped each other get through it.

"It's a matter of always keeping in mind that the person you fell in love with is still the person who's standing in front of you."

Ironically, Hall would eventually find happiness with the man she dumped to marry Dubelko. Deidre had actually been engaged to TV producer Steve Sohmer, whom she had been seeing since 1984, when she and Dubelko fell in love. Instead of being bitter, however, Sohmer was patient, and when he heard Hall and Dubelko had split, he rekindled their romance. It was a situation straight out of the soap opera handbook.

"Steve was the one great love of my life and I knew it the instant I met him," Hall says. "It was the most thrilling, most exciting, most satisfying time. I'd met my mate."

So, why didn't she marry him? Hall blames the demands of their two careers.

"I was very focused on getting into primetime and reaching a lot of career goals that I'd fought hard to achieve. I needed somebody completely flexible and patient, while Steve needed somebody who was completely supportive and able to fit into the high-pressure, demanding job he was in.

"I couldn't be that, he couldn't be who I needed in my life and finally, with this *tremendous* source of frustration, we separated."

When Hall and Sohmer got back together their priorities had changed. They realized they were being given a rare second chance and were determined to make the best of it, beginning with a lavish, storybook wedding that took place on New Year's Eve 1991 near the English village of Shipton-under-Wychwood, where Sohmer maintains an apartment.

Their idyllic life together was about to be sorely tested. For years, Hall had been desperate to be a mother. During her marriage to Dubelko, Deidre had undergone six unsuccessful attempts at artificial insemination. Then, she underwent a half dozen surgical attempts at in vitro fertilization, during the last of which she nearly lapsed into a coma.

By the time she and Sohmer married, doctors had advised Hall to stop trying to conceive or risk potentially serious health complications. Hall was still determined to be a mother, so she and Sohmer discussed adoption. But Steve had another thought—to have a surrogate artificially inseminated with his sperm. "That way," he reasoned, "we could get to know the mother."

While Hall and Sohmer researched surrogacy, Deidre accepted an offer to return to *Days of Our Lives.* Because her character had presumably died in a plane crash, the producers considered bringing her back as a new character. But Hall wouldn't hear of it.

"I said no. I loved Marlena and that's who I wanted to play. So I walked away, they walked away, and the deal fell apart."

But not for long. In 1991, she got her wish and returned as Marlena. Just as Hall was reintroduced to ecstatic *Days* fans, Deidre and Steve were introduced to Robin, a Deidre lookalike who agreed to be their surrogate mother. On August 3, 1992, Robin gave birth to David Atticus Sohmer. Two and a half years later, on January 19, 1995, Robin bore the couple a second child, Tully. Hall and Sohmer were ecstatic to be parents, and Deidre admits that having children has made her change her priorities. Her once all-consuming ambition has been tempered because her career, public image, and fame aren't the most important things in her life anymore.

"I think that's what being a parent is all about—you get over yourself," she laughs.

Just when her life should have been its most peaceful and fulfilling, however, Hall suddenly found herself in a financial quagmire when she was forced to go to court to try and recoup $800,000 she had lent to her cancer-stricken psychoanalyst, who died without repaying the loan. After his death, the family told Deidre that his debt had died with him, effectively telling Hall she was out of luck.

Deidre, however, refused to play victim and sued the doctor's socialite wife and his sons, eventually winning her case and recouping most of her money. But just as that near-disaster was averted, in 1996 Hall slapped a lawsuit on her accountant, charging him with ripping her off for more than $1 million. Unfortunately, the accountant, Robert Houston, had apparently spent much of the money supporting a lavish lifestyle. Most shocking to Deidre was that Houston had used some of the money to finance a failed pin-up calendar business.

At an earlier time, Hall would have been devastated by the loss. But her maturity, combined with the support and strength provided by her family, enabled her to weather this monetary setback with dignified grace. In fact, having a family has put everything in a new perspective.

"I spent years being career-obsessed, driven, focused, and myopic about a career. Before being a parent, it was always a question of *Does it serve my career?* Nowadays, the question is, *Does it serve my family?*

"To tell the truth, I have no more ambition. I have run out of ambition. I don't care if my career ends tomorrow." Hall says, "I've now got everything I've ever wanted in life."

Awards and Accolades: Hall has won the *Soap Opera Digest* Best Actress Award five times, and for 108 straight months was rated number one in *Daytime TV* magazine's popularity poll.

Feuds: Hall has been involved in two public feuds. The first was with costar Crystal Chappell, who had been on the show only three years (as Carly Manning) when she butted heads with *Days*'s reigning diva. Chappell allegedly questioned why Deidre was treated like the set's queen bee, a charge Hall took umbrage with. Eventually, according to printed reports, the two had a screaming match on the set, forcing producers to get involved. They made it clear to Chappell that if they were forced to choose, she would end up the loser.

Hall's other feud was with fellow diva Susan Lucci. Deidre refused to attend the 1994 Daytime Emmy Awards, cohosted by Lucci, after she wasn't asked to participate as a presenter. Sources close to the production said Deidre's lack of an invitation wasn't an oversight. Lucci, who hadn't been nominated that year, had only reluctantly agreed to host the ceremony and knowing that there was no love lost between Hall and Lucci, organizers of the event thought it best to do everything in their power not to upset Susan.

So, when Hall found out she wasn't going to be a presenter, she decided not to attend at all.

Most Notable Real-Life Diva Moments: Playing herself in the TV movie *Never Say Never,* which recounted her unsuccessful struggle to conceive a child and the emotional roller-coaster of hiring a surrogate mother. Some critics accused Hall of exploiting her infertility as a career ploy, but Hall shrugged off the barbs, saying she was doing other women a service by going public with her story.

In 1999, Hall was on hand at FAO Schwartz in New York City to celebrate the launch of a Marlena Evans doll. The diva told reporters, "I do have one at home. I've combed her hair and I've cut her hair and I'm seeing if I can find some clothes for her."

Trivia: Hall's twin, Andrea Hall-Lovell, also appeared on *Days of Our Lives* as Marlena's twin, Samantha. In one shocking plot twist in 1982, Marlena was presumably murdered by the Salem Strangler. Fans were outraged—but the next episode revealed that it was actually Samantha who had been killed.

Div-o-Meter: 10—with a bullet.

SUSAN SEAFORTH HAYES

*Susan Seaforth Hayes's onscreen romance
turned into a real-life love story.*

Crowning Role: Julie Olson Williams on *Days of Our Lives*

Reign: 1968–84, 1990–93, 1994

Character's Most Notable Pursuit: Staying out of the emergency
room while finding true love.

Character's Full Name: Julie Olson Banning Anderson Williams

Husbands: Scott Banning, Bob Anderson, and Doug Williams

Character's Diva-lution: No family was as central to the town of
Salem as the Hortons. Dr. Tom Horton, chief of Internal Medicine at
the local hospital, and his wife, Alice, had a large, fertile brood who
populated the town with memorable characters. Julie's mom was
Tom Horton's daughter Addie, and her father was Ben Olson.

In 1966, Julie became engaged to David Martin, but the wedding was called off when David impregnated Julie's best friend, Susan Martin. David married Susan, and a year later, Julie herself got pregnant after a fling with David. But instead of keeping David Jr., she put the child up for adoption.

Two years later, Julie discovered that Bradley Banning was in fact her son David, so she married Scott Banning, making her son's name David Banning. Her marriage to Scott, however, wasn't meant to be, especially after Doug Williams arrived in Salem in 1970. Although he passed himself off as a nightclub singer, Doug had been the cellmate of Julie's uncle, Bill Horton, who had served time in prison. Doug's intent was to use his considerable charm to con Salem's wealthy lonely ladies.

Meanwhile, Susan Martin still obsessed over Scott, and in an attempt to get him back, she hired Doug to begin an affair with Julie. When Susan later changed her mind, she couldn't convince Doug to stop his seduction of Julie, and Doug and Julie became lovers. By 1971, Julie and Scott's marriage was so rocky that he moved to another city, taking David with him. Around the same time, Julie's mother Addie came back from Paris after Julie's dad, Ben, died.

Julie filed for divorce from Scott so she could marry Doug. Addie, disapproving of the affair, confronted Doug and found herself attracted to him. In 1972, just when Julie's divorce was about to be final, she decided that she and Doug needed to take her son David with them. When it was obvious Doug didn't want to, Julie walked out, leaving Doug to believe she was truly dumping him. She wasn't. Before she could recant, however, Addie proposed to Doug. He accepted and they eloped. Feeling abandoned, Julie withdrew her divorce petition and remained married to Scott. Both Doug and Julie were still in love with each other, but because of their misunderstanding, kept their feelings secret.

Julie's loneliness grew when Scott was killed in 1973. Though she was now available, Doug wasn't. Not only was he married to her mother, but they were expecting a child. Julie's emotions were further complicated when Addie was diagnosed with leukemia. When Addie slipped into a coma, Julie had fantasies of raising her half sister, Hope, with Doug but then Addie made a miraculous recovery.

When Bob Anderson, who owned the company where Scott was killed, divorced his wife, he showered Julie with attention and affection and proposed to her. Julie accepted, not out of love, but due to her desire for financial security. She was still passionately in love with Doug.

Not long afterward, Addie was walking Hope and was hit by a speeding car while crossing the street. Addie managed to push Hope's carriage out of harm's way but was struck and killed by the car. Not only had Julie lost her mother, but she was now married to someone else, unable to be with Doug. Considering her heart was elsewhere, her marriage to Bob faded fast and once again she found herself filing for divorce.

Julie and Doug were on the cusp of being reunited when she discovered she was pregnant with Bob's child. Unwilling to come between Bob and his child, Doug told Julie he didn't love her anymore and insisted she go back to Bob. Instead, Julie lived in Doug's guestroom. After being presumed dead in a car accident, Julie's son, David, suddenly appeared back in Salem. In her joy, Julie fell down a flight of stairs and miscarried. Now that there was no child holding them together, she and Bob promptly divorced.

Now the road was clear for Julie and Doug to be together—almost. In 1976, after announcing their engagement, a woman came to Salem claiming to be looking for her long lost husband, Brent Douglas, which, it turned out, was Doug Williams's real name. In the end, the woman admitted she'd been lying and that Doug wasn't really her husband after all, leaving him free to finally marry Julie.

Doug and Julie were married in October 1976. Less than a year later, trouble began brewing in the guise of Larry Atwood, a sculptor who became enamored with Julie. His obsession led him to frame Doug on drug charges. While Doug was in jail, Larry made advances toward Julie. When she rejected him, he raped her. Out of shame, she didn't tell anyone. When Doug was released, she rejected him. He, naturally, thought it was because he'd been in jail. Then he heard, wrongly as it happened, that Julie and Larry had had an affair. Unable to bear Doug believing her unfaithful, she told him the truth.

Furious, Doug went to confront Larry, only to find him dead. Julie was arrested for the murder but was acquitted after one of Larry's associates confessed to the crime.

Things were quiet for Julie until 1979, when a faulty oven seriously burned her, leaving her badly scarred. When the first round of skin grafts didn't take, she was convinced Doug wouldn't want her anymore so she fled to Mexico and got a quickie divorce.

By the time she recovered physically and emotionally, Doug had gotten married to Lee Dumonde. Julie decided to stop feeling sorry for herself and to fight Lee for Doug. Doug realized he had never fallen out of love with Julie, and he asked Lee for a divorce. She not only refused, she hired a hit man to kill Julie. The attempt failed, and the hit man left Salem. But Lee managed to hang on to Doug by allegedly having a stroke.

In 1981, the killer returned, intent on earning the $150,000 Lee had promised him for killing Julie. But when he tried to kill Julie and then Bill, Lee leaped from her wheelchair, grabbed a gun, and killed the hit man. Doug had Lee committed and moved back in with Julie.

Shortly before Julie and Doug were to be remarried, Lee was released. She planned to kidnap Julie, but her plot backfired. Julie and Doug were once again husband and wife.

Over the next couple of years, Julie faded into the Salem background as the town's younger generation took center stage. In April 1984, Julie left Salem and wasn't heard from again until 1990. Other than being caught in an explosion and surviving emergency surgery, the next three years were relatively quiet. She left in 1993 to join Doug in Switzerland and made a brief visit in May 1994, after the death of Dr. Tom Horton.

Currently, Julie and Doug make their home in Florida.

Of Special Note: Ted Corday, who created *Days of Our Lives* with Irna Phillips and Allan Chase, died shortly after the serial debuted. His wife, Betty Corday, took over as executive producer and held the reins for the next twenty years.

Real-Life Soap Opera: Susan was born in Oakland, California, on July 11, 1943. When she was only two years old, her father walked out on her and her mother, a radio actress named Elizabeth Harrower (Harrower later became one of *Days*'s head writers). Susan remembers growing up poor in her grandmother's boardinghouse in an area rife with crime and drug use.

Her one refuge was the theater. She made her first stage appearance when she was just four, then found steady work in television. She made the transition to adult roles with relative ease, making several appearances on *Divorce Court* as the "other woman." It was a part she found herself playing in real life, too, admittedly wasting many years dating married men. "I see now what I was doing," she says candidly.

In the 1960s, Susan put her career on a back burner while she became involved in politics. She returned to acting in time to be cast in the role of Julie Olson on the then-new *Days of Our Lives,* where she would become a daytime fixture. It wasn't necessarily the career she thought she'd have, but one she accepted gladly.

"I wanted to move into nighttime TV, but it was apparent the quality just wasn't there in primetime," she notes.

And although primetime may not have come a-calling, Susan has found a niche for herself in her first love, theater. With her husband, Bill Hayes, Susan has appeared in *Same Time, Next Year; A Christmas Carol,* and the extremely popular two-character drama *Love Letters.* Independently, she starred in a revival of Neil Simon's *Rumors* with former *Santa Barbara* star David Haskell.

After leaving *Days of Our Lives,* Susan made brief appearances on *The Young and the Restless* and portrayed a district attorney on *Sunset Beach* in April 1999. She also appeared in some feature films, including *The Dream Machine* and *Wrestling with God.* While still living in Los Angeles, Susan also acted as a celebrity tour guide for the Gene Autry Museum of Western Heritage.

Currently, she and Bill reside in Arizona, where they run an alcohol rehabilitation home.

Most Notable Real-Life Diva Moment: Marrying her costar after a torrid on-set romance. In 1970, when Bill Hayes joined the cast of *Days,* he was, in his words, "emotionally exhausted." He was recently divorced from his wife of twenty-three years and had custody of their five children. Susan was involved in a long-term relationship with local L.A. newscaster Hal Fishman. On the set, Bill and Susan became friends—which was all Bill says he was ready for at first. As the romance between their characters developed, however, Bill and Susan realized it was more than just role-playing.

Despite their eighteen-year age difference—Susan was 37, Bill 55—they fell in love. "Once we became lovers, I never had eyes for anyone else," Susan says. Despite their involvement, Susan and Bill didn't live together and waited to get married until October 1974, after Bill's youngest child graduated from high school.

Two years to the month later, Julie and Doug were married in what was one of daytime's most talked-about weddings at the time. After that, Bill and Susan were the darlings of the talk-show set and later, after leaving *Days,* turned their enduring popularity into a career by performing together in plays and nightclub acts to houses packed with their legion of loyal fans.

Div-o-Meter: 3—Susan, and Julie for that matter, was always way too nice to compete with the likes of fellow *Days* divas Deidre Hall, Patricia Barry, or Susan Flannery.

The literate and lovely Liz Hubbard.

ELIZABETH HUBBARD

Crowning Role: Lucinda Walsh on *As the World Turns*

Reign: April 1984–present

Other Notable Roles: Dr. Althea Davis on *The Doctors* (1964–82)

What Liz Says About Lucinda: "I'd like to get her back in the office and have her rattle her saber."

Character's Most Notable Pursuit: Interfering in the lives of those she loves most by scheming behind their backs, often with the help of private detectives

Character's Full Name: Lucinda Esteban Guest Walsh Dixon Stenbeck

Character's Occupation: CEO of Worldwide Industries; owner of RiverWalk

Husbands: Jacobo Esteban, James Walsh, Martin Guest, John Dixon, and James Stenbeck

Character's Real Name: Mary Ellen Walters

Character's Diva-lution: Lucinda Walsh came to Oakdale by way of Peoria, Illinois. As a young girl, she was emotionally abandoned by her mother, Gloria, whose new husband, George Keller, had no interest in raising Lucinda.

By the time Lucy got to Oakdale, her past had more twists and turns than a gyroscope. Fiercely protective of her family, she is the mother of three children—Sierra, Lily, and Bianca, the latter two adopted. She had originally come to Oakdale with Lily, who, it was eventually revealed, was the natural daughter of Iva Snyder. Meanwhile, Lucinda's birth-daughter, Sierra Esteban, the product of her first marriage, was living in the war-torn country of Montega. Lucy had no contact with her daughter, because when Esteban found out that Lucinda was in love with another man, he told her to get out of Montega and leave their daughter behind—or he would kill her lover.

In 1990, Connor Jamison Walsh and her younger brother, Evan, came to Oakdale bent on destroying Lucinda, who had been married to their grandfather and whom they blamed for their father's suicide. They stole Walsh Enterprises away from Lucinda. Refusing to roll over, Lucinda established a new company called Worldwide Industries, which became Walsh Enterprises's chief competitor.

Lucinda married John Dixon. Although they were passionately in love, both were headstrong and unable to compromise, so they eventually divorced. They remain close friends.

In 1993, Lucinda learned she had half siblings from her mother's marriage to George Keller—architect Royce Keller and artist Neal Alcott. But shortly after her arrival in Oakdale, Neal was killed.

During the murder trial, Royce told the court that his name was Roger and that he was the murderer—even though it really was an accident. Turns out Royce was suffering from multiple personality disorder and had three competing personalities—Royce, Roger, and a little boy named Dooley. Lucy paid to have Royce treated for his disorder and eventually the three personalities fused.

Meanwhile, Lucinda's detectives learned that Royce had a twin that was given up at birth. Lucinda tracked down her half sister, Samantha Markham, a con artist and art forger who tried to swindle Lucinda before turning over a new leaf. Before leaving town under mysterious circumstances, Sam was reunited with Georgia Tucker, the daughter she had abandoned at birth. Lucinda was left to play "Auntie Lou" to her teenaged niece.

Lucinda got involved with yet another wrong man—the notorious villain James Stenbeck—with whom she'd once had a child. Lucinda had been told her child was stillborn, but years later, James claimed that Oakdale's new district attorney, David Allen (later David Stenbeck), was their long lost child. It was later revealed that Lucinda was not David's mother, though he was a Stenbeck through and through. Lucy ended up marrying James after discovering that her son-in-law, Holden, shot David and left him for dead. When James found out, he tried to kill Holden but wounded Lucy instead. Lucy took a long trip to Florida to rehabilitate from her injuries. After several months away, she came back with a vengeance, just in time to help orchestrate David Stenbeck's downfall.

Of Special Note: Unhappy with the direction her storyline was taking, Hubbard shocked fans and her *As the World Turns* producers by opting not to re-sign her contract in March 1999. Newly appointed executive producer Christopher Goutman was able to lure her back, however, and Hubbard made a triumphant return to the soap in August 1999.

Real-Life Soap Opera: Born and raised in New York, Elizabeth came from anything but a showbiz family. "No, my mother was a doctor. My father was at Columbia College. There was nothing of the theater in our background," she says. If anything, academia seemed a more likely career path.

"I was very lucky," notes Elizabeth, who as a child was a voracious reader. "I had a very literate mother. I remember being 9 or 11 and saying to my mom, 'What should I read?' And my mom said to me, 'Have you read Proust?'"

After graduating cum laude from Radcliffe, Elizabeth was accepted to study at the Royal Academy of Dramatic Art in London, and was the first American to receive the school's silver medal.

She returned to New York after completing her education. In 1964, she was cast in the central role of Dr. Althea Davis on *The Doctors,* where she challenged conventional stereotypes and proved that women could have high profile careers, brains, and passion.

Over the years, Hubbard has appeared in numerous Broadway dramas, including *The Physicists* (for which she received the Clarence Derwent Award), *Joe Egg, Children! Children!, John Gabriel Borkman, Look Back in Anger,* and Noel Coward's *Present Laughter,* opposite George C. Scott.

Although television audiences know her mainly as a dramatic actress, Hubbard is also a gifted singer and has appeared in a variety of musicals, such as *Dance a Little Closer, A Time for Singing,* and a musical version of *I Remember Mama* with Liv Ullmann.

It is, however, her role as Lucinda Walsh that Hubbard is closest to. "Lucinda helps me make decisions," she admits. "Quite often, people will say to me, 'Oh, you helped me so much because Lucinda helps me make decisions.' Well, I say, 'Lucinda helps me make decisions, too.' I've used her in a tough spot—*Hmm. What the hell would Lucinda do?*"

When she's not acting, Hubbard is active in a variety of causes and enjoys writing and traveling. She is the proud mother of Jeremy Bennett, a TV reporter in New Jersey.

Awards and Accolades: Elizabeth won her first Emmy for her work in *The Doctors* and a second one for her portrayal of Edith Wilson in *First Ladies' Diaries*. She has received eight additional Daytime Emmy nominations for Outstanding Actress, ten *Soap Opera Digest* Award nominations, and four *Soap Opera Update* MVP Awards.

Causes: Hubbard is involved with the Women's Commission on Women and Children Refugees and Seconding the First, a coalition of performers and others whose mission is to bring attention to the threat censorship poses to all Americans.

Most Notable Real-Life Diva Moment: In 1993, Hubbard flew to war-torn Bosnia as part of a humanitarian mission. Although her soap character may have been acquainted with Montega, a fictional country in turmoil, Hubbard had the opportunity to experience the real thing.

Concerned by events she saw in the news and appalled by the stories of suffering, Hubbard joined a group called the Women's Commission for Refugee Women and Children. The group's mission was to find out, firsthand, what the living conditions were really like. "After looking at photos of the suffering in Bosnia, I just had to go there," Hubbard explained at the time. "I had to do anything I could. Just to talk, to listen. God knows I can listen."

Trivia: In 1974, Hubbard received the first Emmy ever awarded for Best Actress in a Daytime Drama. Macdonald Carey of *Days of Our Lives* won for Best Actor.

Div-o-Meter: 9—For taking on producers and rebel forces with equal verve.

SUSAN LUCCI

Susan Lucci calls Erica Kane "the greatest role ever written for a woman."

Crowning Role: Erica Kane on *All My Children*

Reign: 1970–present

What Susan Says About Erica: "I think Erica is happiest when she is in love. I would love to see Erica head over heels in love again. That does lead to marriage for Erica."

Character's Most Notable Pursuit: Finding the perfect man— and seemingly having them all in the process

Character's Full Name: Erica Kane Martin Brent Cudahy Chandler Montgomery Chandler Marick

Husbands: Jeff Martin, Phil Brent, Tom Cudahy, Adam Chandler, Travis Montgomery, and Dimitri Marick

Erica Kane

All My Children has made a reputation for tackling social issues, often with Erica Kane taking the lead. In 1979, Erica's third husband, Tom Cudahy, discovered she had been taking birth control pills behind his back, effectively ending the marriage. Although to millions of woman watching, it was a slice of life, it was controversial stuff for a network. Just as it was when Erica made history by having daytime's first legal abortion.

Love her or hate her, it's this kind of independent thinking that has fans still tuning in each day to watch her, thirty years later.

Character's Diva-lution: Although a psychologist might explain that all of Erica's manipulations, scheming, and backstabbing over the years is simply a result of the deep-seated need to be loved and an equally firmly rooted insecurity, all the residents of Pine Valley know is that Erica Kane is not a woman to be fooled with—or to turn your back on.

By the time *All My Children* debuted, Erica—a central character from day one—was carrying the emotional scars of having been abandoned by her father when she was a child. Her desperate need for love showed itself early, when she eloped with medical student Jeff Martin in 1971. In a pattern that would repeat itself with dizzying regularity, that marriage soon crumbled.

Four years later, she found herself pregnant and married the baby's father, Phil Brent. But her happiness at the prospect of being a mother was shattered when she miscarried, which led her to a nervous breakdown and a second divorce. Erica eventually bounced back from her depression and got engaged to her mother's close friend, Nick Davis. After she contracted viral pneumonia, however, she dumped Nick in favor of Tom Cudahay, who, not so coincidentally, was also her rival Brooke English's object of desire.

After Erica and Tom married in 1978, she deceived him by secretly taking birth control pills. Tom was anxious to start a family, but Erica had other plans. Then she opened a disco in Pine Valley without consulting her husband; two years later, the club fell victim to waning disco fever. Depressed and feeling as if life was passing her by, Erica packed her bags and headed for Hollywood.

After failing to launch a movie career, Erica returned to Pine Valley and began secretly working as a fashion model. When Tom found out about her latest deception, he divorced Erica. She wasn't too broken up about it because by then she had two powerful men chasing her—rival cosmetics tycoons Kent Bogard and Brandon Kingsley, the man who made her a fashion star, but her embarrassment of romantic riches turned sour. First, she discovered that Brandon was married with children and had no intention of leaving his family. Then she learned that Kent was having an affair with the woman Erica believed to be her half sister, Silver Kane. Soon after discovering their affair, Erica accidentally shot Kent. Not surprisingly, the police believed it was murder.

Suddenly finding herself on the lam, Erica disguised herself as a nun. She was caught and tossed in jail, but eventually got out. Free at last, Erica focused on her career goals. She opened her own cosmetics company. She also wrote a bestselling autobiography, *Raising Kane.*

Now the toast of the town, Erica fell in love with writer Mike Roy, but left him to marry Adam Chandler. At the time, Chandler was a movie producer who promised to make Erica a star. He didn't.

Instead, he faked his own death as a sort of loyalty test. After Erica failed by immediately going back to Mike, Adam reappeared. She, however, turned down Adam's promises and money to stay with Mike. It was too little, too late—Mike was killed (presumably) and Erica lost what she believed may have been her one chance at true happiness.

Then she met Jeremy Hunter. There was one little snag to their relationship—Hunter was celibate. Oh, and did we mention that his former lover also happened to be his stepmother? While Erica was trying to figure that one out, she entered a new business venture, becoming editor of *Tempo* magazine. Life with Jeremy fell apart after he was sent to prison and rejected Erica's offer to bust him out by swooping down with a helicopter.

In 1987, a new man entered Erica's life—politician Travis Montgomery. Erica got pregnant but kept it a secret, not wanting to ruin Travis's campaign for office. Just as she was happily planning her wedding to Travis, she met his brother, Jackson. Sparks flew. But she married Travis anyway, and gave birth to their daughter, Bianca, in 1988.

Their marriage was troubled, especially after Travis's scheme to arrange his own kidnapping in order to bilk an insurance firm of the ransom money backfired, resulting in Bianca's abduction instead. Erica fled Pine Valley and unwittingly fell into a romance with the kidnapper. She eventually came back to give her marriage another chance. Unfortunately, Travis had lost his memory and couldn't remember who Erica was, so he went back to his first wife, Barbara. What nobody realized was that Travis was suffering from a brain tumor. That same year, Erica's father, Eric, came back to Pine Valley just long enough to betray her to her worst enemy, Natalie Hunter.

Feeling emotionally battered and bruised, Erica turned to Travis's brother, Jackson. When Jack proposed, however, Erica hesitated due to her daughter Bianca's desire to see her parents reunited. When Bianca contracted a near-fatal illness, Erica and Travis decided to remarry, for the sake of their child. Things fell apart quickly, however, and Erica went back to Jackson. When Jackson found out Erica was still sleeping with his brother, he called the relationship off for good.

Because Jackson admitted to their affair during the custody hearing, Travis won custody of Bianca and moved with her to Seattle. Meanwhile, Adam Chandler informed Erica they had never been legally divorced and she consented to a faked "remarriage" in order to avoid a public scandal. On the business front, she struggled to keep her cosmetics company from being taken over, only to fall passionately in love with the man trying to take her company—Dimitri Marick.

By 1993, Dimitri and Erica were together, although she had to fake a little amnesia to keep him. But trouble arrived on their doorstep in the guise of Kendall Hart, the daughter Erica gave up for adoption at age fourteen, after becoming pregnant as the result of a rape. Even more conniving than Erica, Kendall told her mother that she, too, had been raped—by Dimitri. In a moment of fury, Erica stabbed Dimitri in the chest with a letter opener.

In 1994, Erica stood trial and Kendall lied on the witness stand. Her perjury was eventually discovered and Kendall was sent to jail. Attempted murder notwithstanding, Erica and Dimitri finally married on New Year's Eve, 1994. Erica launched a new talk show but became addicted to painkillers after hurting her back during a modeling assignment. While under the influence of drugs, she was seduced by her doctor. Then she crashed her car. Finally, Dimitri asked for a divorce.

After making a spectacle of herself in public, Erica finally admitted her problem and checked into rehab. Once clean and sober, she reconciled with Dimitri, then set out to expose Dr. Kinder's malpractice. Realizing he had been found out, Kinder kidnapped Bianca, but during the abduction, he fell down some stairs. Believing him dead, Erica buried his body.

Once again, Erica got pregnant and once again she miscarried—this time on the day she was set to remarry Dimitri. She was thrown even further when she discovered that Dimitri had a one-night stand with another woman, Maria, and might be the father of Maria's baby. Although Dimitri was not, in fact, the child's father, someone had falsified medical records to show that he was. The real father was Dimitri's brother, Edmund.

One cold and stormy night, Erica confronted Maria, who was staying at a cabin in the woods. The stress of the encounter caused Maria to go into premature labor and Erica delivered the baby. She intended to take the child to the hospital, but on route, she skidded off an icy road and into a lake. The child was presumed dead.

Some time afterward, Erica discovered that the baby was miraculously saved by a woman who had taken the infant girl in. Erica claimed the baby, but rather than tell Maria that her daughter was alive, Erica instead pretended that she adopted the little girl from Russia. Dimitri discovered Erica's lie, and Erica eventually returned the child to its rightful parents, Maria and Edmund. Erica was charged with kidnapping.

After spending most of 1997 in jail, Erica discovered Bianca was anorexic. She was desperate to get out and help her daughter. After Edmund came forward to speak on her behalf, Erica was paroled. She gave Bianca a job, in hopes of turning her daughter's life around.

In 1998, Erica and Jackson tried one more time to build a life together and once again planned to be married. Their future was jeopardized by the return of Mike Roy, who claimed to be part of a spy ring. Jackson didn't believe his story and warned Erica to stay away from Mike. In the end, Erica decided she wanted to be with Jack, but she agreed to sleep with Mike one last time as a farewell gesture, as it were. Jack found out and broke off the engagement for good. Mike left town, leaving Erica all alone again.

In 1999, Erica sustained devastating injuries in a car crash, including severe damage to her face, which forced her to wear a *Phantom of the Opera*–type mask to hide her injuries.

She regained her looks and, ironically, began an affair with the much-younger David Hayward, the doctor who caused the accident that scarred her.

And so it goes.

Of Special Note: Lucci's daughter, Liza Huber, is following in her mother's formidable footsteps, currently starring in the new NBC soap *Passions.* "I've been working very, very hard to become a professional actress," says Huber. "We knew if I decided to do a soap, it would be more difficult for me than someone else. There would be harsher criticism and more attention. But Susan Lucci is my mom, my best friend. I neither hide it nor flaunt it."

Real-Life Soap Opera: Even as a child, Susan Lucci had a thing about television in general and soap operas in particular, enjoying shows such as *Search for Tomorrow* and *Love of Life.*

"I would sneak down the stairs at night," says Lucci, "and stay on the stairs and watch the television in the living room [that] my parents were watching. Since I can remember, I wanted to be an actress. My father really encouraged me to dream my dreams and never let anything deter me."

After Lucci graduated from Garden City High School, she enrolled at Marymount College in Tarrytown, New York, to study drama. But her would-be career almost never happened. During her senior year, she was seriously injured when the car she was riding in, driven by her then-fiancé, hit another car, causing Susan to be thrown face-first into the windshield.

"I felt no pain, but I knew I was hurt, and I felt something dripping down my face," she says. "When we got to the emergency room, the nurses were talking about me in the past tense, saying, 'Oh, I could tell she was a beautiful girl.' One of them saw my engagement ring and said, 'Gee, honey, do you think he'll still marry you?'"

The plastic surgeon who attended to Lucci made sure she wouldn't be scarred for life. "I completely recovered," she says gratefully. And she still planned on marrying her fiancé—until a twist of fate changed those plans. During the summer of 1965, after completing her first year of college, Susan got a job working as a waitress at the Garden City Hotel. The hotel's chef was an Austrian named Helmut Huber, who took one look at Susan and lost his heart.

"The first time I saw Susie, it hit me," says Huber. "Still today, she walks in a room, and I just light up."

Lucci immediately noticed Helmut, too. "I thought at the time he was an attractive older man." Not only was Lucci engaged, but she was also leery of their nine-year age difference, which seemed like an eternity to the teenager.

In 1968, Lucci held her engagement party at the Garden City Hotel, and as fate would have it, Helmut was there. Although he was now working for a different hotel chain, he happened to be visiting friends.

"My parents invited him to join the party," says Lucci. She found herself still attracted to Huber, who, she says, "leaned over to my mother and said, 'This thing between Susie and this boy is never going to last.' I heard about that much later. And my mother agreed with him, but she didn't tell me that."

Mother, it seems, does know best. Lucci did indeed break up with her fiancé and eventually began dating the persistent Helmut, whom she married on September 13, 1969. And although Erica changes husbands like she changes perfumes, Lucci's real-life marriage is still going strong after thirty years.

Although Lucci had gotten a small taste of the business when she came to New York, an independent film and a bit part on *As the World Turns* were the sum total of her experience before she auditioned for a pivotal role on the planned new soap *All My Children*. If there was one thing she did know, however, it was how to be a feisty, head-strong teenager—which was how the casting breakdown described Erica Kane.

"I was a self-centered, haughty girl," Susan admits.

She got the part and daytime television would never be the same. *TV Guide* once called Erica Kane "unequivocally the most famous soap opera character in the history of daytime TV."

Unlike some soap actors who get restless and feel the need to leave the nest to pursue other career options, Lucci has steadfastly kept her *All My Children* base while spreading her acting wings. Thanks to her popularity as Erica, Lucci has been able to successfully make the transition to primetime via television movies, including *Seduced and Betrayed, Ebbie, French Silk, Between Love and Hate, Blood on Her Hands, The Bride in Black, Lady Mobster,* and *Mafia Princess.* She has also shown her willingness to spoof herself with appearances on *Saturday Night Live* and in a series of commercials for the sugar substitute Sweet One.

In 1990, Susan appeared in a story arc on *Dallas,* a match that seemed made in television heaven. "It was just one of those wonderful phone calls," Lucci said, where they asked, "'Will you allow us to write the first four episodes of *Dallas* and shoot it in Paris?' I mean, Let me think about it, you know—for about 30 seconds!"

In the series, she played a backstabbing, double-dealing widow named Sheila Foley, whose oilman husband went bankrupt and committed suicide after OPEC cut prices. Determined to avenge his death, Sheila arrived in Paris for OPEC meetings, kidnapped Bobby's new wife, and assumed her identity in order to infiltrate the group.

Shooting in France proved to be an eye-opening experience, but not in the way she had anticipated. Because *All My Children* didn't air in Paris, none of the locals knew who Lucci was.

"I thought it would be a relief," she noted, and then laughingly admitted, "It's not. It's very strange! I mean, I've been doing this my whole adult life. I've been on top of the Alps in Austria and been recognized in ski clothes. And suddenly here in Paris, it's only the American tourists who recognize me but the French people all recognize Patrick [Duffy]. That's a little odd for me."

Another area that Susan feels removed from is feature film. "There seem to be a lot of wonderful actresses working in films, and I don't know if there's room for anyone else," she says candidly. "And so far, no one's breaking down my door for feature films, but certainly if the opportunity were there, I'd love to do it. But I also think television has more parts for women."

Although Lucci admits it might have been nice to be a movie star, one of her goals has simply been to get back onstage. A talented musical comedy performer in college, Susan sought an opportunity to strut her stuff on Broadway. She signed on to replace Bernadette Peters in the Broadway revival of *Annie Get Your Gun* for three weeks in 1999.

Just as she continues to be content going to work every day as Erica Kane. "The truth is, I'm happy. This is one of those once-in-a-lifetime parts—I think Erica's the greatest role ever written for a woman. That's one reason I've stayed."

Awards and Accolades: Out of nineteen Daytime Emmy nominations as Outstanding Actress in a Drama Series, Lucci won the award once, in 1999. She has also received a People's Choice Award (1992), the *Soap Opera Digest* Editor's Award for Outstanding Contribution to Daytime Television (1988), a *Soap Opera Digest* Award for Outstanding Actress (1993), a Crystal Apple Award (1994), the Italian-American Welfare League's "Woman of the Year," and the American Academy of Achievement Award (1991). The readers of *People* magazine voted her Best Soap Actress in 1985, and she won *Canadian TV Guide*'s People's Choice Award for Best Soap Actress in 1989.

Cause: Susan says, "My favorite charity is the Little Flower Children's Services of New York. They provide shelter, education, and love and care for abandoned children."

Feuds: When you've been on a show for almost thirty years and are considered an icon in the history of daytime, what would there be to feud about? Turns out the answer is as old as *All About Eve.*

The first rumblings of discontent came after the writers introduced the character of Kendall, the daughter Erica had put up for adoption as a teenager. In the beginning, it seemed as if the onscreen mother and daughter would get along famously.

Gellar recalls, "I remember on my first day when I walked into the rehearsal hall, Susan and Michael [Nader] were rehearsing a scene. I was very nervous. I kept thinking, 'What if I'm really bad and they fire me?' I just snuck in the back and tried to blend in with the coffee machine, when all of a sudden, Susan said, 'Hold it, we need to stop for a minute.'

"Then she walked over to me and said, 'Congratulations! I'm very glad you're here.' She put her arm around me and said, 'Don't worry, nobody bites.' And then she introduced me to everyone who was there. She really did help me and always made sure I was okay during my first couple of weeks when I was still unsettled."

Even so, others noted that Lucci seemed bent on doing little things to keep Sarah off balance. "For example," says one set source, "she would play a scene one way during rehearsal then abruptly change it when the cameras were rolling. Then when Sarah would stop short, confused, Susan would chastise her, telling her she should really be more professional and learn her lines before shooting a scene.

"Susan would also make cutting little remarks about Sarah's acting and, a few times, Sarah was reduced to tears. The rest of the cast thought Susan's behavior was appalling and that's when the first stories began leaking about Susan being a bitch."

The real problems, however, began a year after Gellar's arrival. One report noted that the first noticeable signs of tension occurred during a rehearsal when Lucci accused Sarah of trying to upstage her—not knowing the director had instructed Gellar to up the emotional ante. It also didn't help that Gellar was now being referred to as "baby Erica." Add to that an Emmy nomination her first year out for Outstanding Younger Actress—the same year Lucci failed to be nominated while costar Julia Barr was—and the stage was set.

"The truth is," says a show associate, "Susan was against the idea of the Kendall storyline to begin with because she didn't really want Erica to be seen as the mother of a daughter in her twenties. Ironically, one of the ways the producers convinced Susan to accept the plot was to convince her that this was the storyline that would finally win her the Emmy."

All of a sudden, the woman who had been known for never abusing her power seemed to be wielding it at will, most notably in the highly publicized dismissal of the show's hairdresser. The point of no return, however, came when Gellar was nominated for her second Daytime Emmy for Outstanding Younger Actress. Although she had lost in the same category for the 1993–94 season, this time out she was the odds-on favorite to win, exacerbating the already volatile situation.

"They were just a bad mix," says one observer. "Sarah loved being the center of attention and she wasn't shy about how her career was heating up." And although it got to the point where Susan and Sarah weren't speaking offcamera, they still did their jobs. "They would be professional and perform their scenes together, then leave and not say a word once the cameras stopped rolling."

At one point, Lucci did not appear in scenes with Gellar for nearly six weeks.

Even before the Emmy ceremony took place, Gellar had decided that win or lose, it was time to leave Pine Valley. As expected, Gellar won—and as equally expected, Lucci did not. Just three days after her Emmy win, Gellar announced her departure from *All My Children*.

When asked today about her relationship with Lucci, Gellar, who has gone on to achieve fame in primetime through *Buffy the Vampire Slayer* and in films such as *I Know What You Did Last Summer* and *Cruel Intentions,* is candid.

"It wasn't an easy time in my life. Susan and I didn't have the most amazing relationship; we were not best friends and we're never going to be. Basically, the best I can say is that we worked together, on top of each other, for so long, that problems were inevitable.

"I denied it for a long time because that's what you're supposed to do, but it also wasn't as bad as people made it out to be. The thing I said to her, that I was not competing against her, was the truth. She was in the leading actress category and I was in the younger actress category. And let's be honest; leading actress is a much more difficult category.

"And you don't work alone—I won for scenes submitted with her; for work we did together. She's a superstar."

And a very human one, at that.

Most Notable Real-Life Diva Moment: Making a career out of having gone o for 18 when nominated for a Daytime Emmy.

What began as a streak of unfortunate luck became a tragedy of operatic proportions with each passing year. And like any good tragic heroine, Lucci underscored her plight with a couple of well-timed scenes: At the 1982 awards banquet, she pounded the table in rage when *One Life to Live*'s Robin Strasser was announced as best actress. Then in 1983, she stormed from the room in tears after losing out to fellow *All My Children* costar Dorothy Lyman.

Despite those outbursts, Lucci maintained, "Sure I was disappointed. But winning the Emmy was never the focal point of my life. The work—acting—really is the point, and that's not just rhetoric. I don't begrudge anyone for having won."

And although her losing streak became doffer for late-night talk-show humor, those closest to Susan saw another side.

"A lot of people thought it was a joke," says *One Life to Live*'s Erika Slezak, a five-time Emmy winner. "Susan never thought it was. It hurt."

Lucci's mother, Jean, recalls that after each loss, Susan would call her crying. "And I'd say, 'Susan, you have such a wonderful husband and wonderful children. You're happy, and come on now, life goes on just the same.' And between tears she'd say, 'Yes, I know, Mom.'"

The question of why Lucci never won became a popular guessing game among television insiders. Some suggested that Susan was the victim of peer jealousy because of her popularity and salary—reportedly the highest in daytime. Others pointed to the fact that Erica Kane wasn't a victim and therefore didn't show the vulnerability the blue ribbon panel of judges seemed to prefer. There were also those who blamed the judging system itself, in which actors submit two episodes for consideration.

Thomas O'Neil, author of the 1992 book *The Emmys,* lays the problem at Lucci's own feet, saying the episodes Susan submitted were akin to "Wagnerian operatic scenes. In the episodes she sent in last year, she was crying 75 percent of the time. She drowned her chances in a tsunami of tears."

So much attention was paid to how desperately Susan wanted an Emmy that some of her peers responded with pique. Elizabeth Hubbard, who plays *As the World Turns*'s resident diva, Lucinda Walsh, tartly noted, "It's extraordinary to think that a person could win just because she wanted it so much. Someone once said that Richard Nixon was elected only because he wanted it so much that the American people gave it to him. Maybe a sticky wheel does get the grease."

Whatever the reason, 1999 finally proved to be Lucci's year. Mainly on the strength of her performance in Bianca's anorexia story-line, Lucci finally won over the Emmy judges. At the Daytime Emmy Awards ceremony on May 21, presenter Shemar Moore from *The Young and the Restless* opened the envelope and announced the winner for Outstanding Actress. "The streak is over!" he yelled, "Susan Lucci!"

Lucci accepted her award in front of a standing ovation of 5,600 present at the Theater in Madison Square Garden.

Historical Footnote: Angela Lansbury, with 0 wins out of 16 nominations (12 for *Murder, She Wrote*), is a close runner-up to Lucci in the Emmy record books.

Div-o-Meter: Off the charts.

Lucci's Second Generation

Growing up as the daughter of television's most famous soap actress who stars as daytime's most notorious character wasn't really that different from most other kids, says Liza Huber, Susan Lucci's offspring.

"She was my mommy. It was just her job. I was either in dance class or horseback riding or hanging out with friends. And I have a European father, so if I had a free moment I was doing something productive. I owe a lot of my success to him."

As a result, Huber admits she still doesn't watch much television, although hopefully others will be watching her. Hoping to establish a name for herself away from her mother's considerable shadow, Liza moved to Los Angeles and, as fate would have it, landed a role on NBC's much-touted new soap, *Passions.*

In the serial, Huber plays beautiful socialite Gwen Hotchkiss. But make no mistake—this is not Erica redux. "She's a hopeless romantic, a quality we've all shared," notes Liza. "She's also real and intelligent. She's down to earth, not snobby—a very non-clichéd rich girl."

As for mom, Lucci admits, "I had apprehensions, sure. But she just jumped in and loved acting so much, and I could see the passion in her."

No pun intended, we're sure.

ROBIN MATTSON

*Robin Mattson: Her Janet from
Another Planet came down to Earth
when she found true love.*

Crowning Role: Janet Green on *All My Children*

Reign: 1994–present

Other Notable Roles: Hope Bauer on *Guiding Light* (1976–77);
Heather Webber on *General Hospital* (1980–83); Delia Ryan on
Ryan's Hope (1984); and Gina Capwell on *Santa Barbara* (1985–93)

Character's Most Notable Pursuit: Being a thorn in everyone's
side

Character's Occupations: Accountant, bookkeeper, and secretary

Character's Full Name: Janet Marlowe Green Dillon

Husbands: Axel Green and Trevor Dillon

Character's Diva-lution: Janet Marlowe first came to Pine Valley in 1991 in search of her look-alike sister, Natalie. Carrying a boulder-sized chip on her shoulder, Janet coveted everything Natalie had, including her fiancé, Trevor Dillon. Feeling she deserved the life Natalie had, Janet kidnapped her sister, tossed her down a well, and assumed her identity.

Though some suspected this wasn't the real Natalie, Trevor was oblivious. He married Janet, who quickly became pregnant. When Natalie returned and Janet was finally revealed to be an imposter, Janet was sent to prison. But before long, she escaped. While on the lam, she killed Will Cortlandt with a crowbar and once again kidnapped Natalie. Just as she was about to kill her sister, however, Janet went into labor and Natalie ended up delivering the baby—a girl named Amanda. As she was being sent back to prison, Janet let Trevor and Natalie adopt the baby.

Knowing the only way to get out of prison was to follow the rules, Janet became a model prisoner. Because of her exemplary record, she was offered the chance of early parole if she would undergo an experimental cosmetic surgery procedure, which would conveniently give her a new face. She agreed.

As soon as she was released, Janet—now going by the name Jane Cox—returned to Pine Valley intent on winning Trevor back. (Natalie had died as the result of a car accident.) When Laurel Banning discovered her true identity, Janet tried to kill Laurel by tampering with her brakes. When that failed, Janet tried to smother Laurel while she was in the hospital recovering from her injuries.

Trevor, like a moth drawn to a flame, proposed to Jane. But the marriage was thwarted when Jane's true identity was finally revealed.

Trevor and Laurel fell in love and planned to be wed, and Janet hatched a plan to bomb the church where their wedding ceremony was supposed to take place. Then, in a scene straight out of *The Bad Seed,* Janet was hit by lightning and presumed killed.

Ha!

Janet had merely been blown into the nearby woods. She was found by artist Pierce Riley, who took her in and nurtured her back to health. Because of his kindness, Janet fell in love with him.

Trevor, meanwhile, married Laurel, who soon turned up dead. Not surprisingly, Janet was accused of the murder. Surprisingly, though, she was proved innocent when the real killer was revealed. Janet's plan for a joyful reunion with Pierce was shattered, however, when she learned he was now in love with Brooke English, the town saint.

Meanwhile, as she grew older, Amanda became curious about Janet and discovered the truth about her unsavory past deeds. Morbidly, Amanda went to see the well where Janet had imprisoned Natalie and accidentally fell into the well herself. When Janet found Amanda and bravely tried to rescue her, she, too, fell in. Finally, Trevor saved them both, just as the well began to cave in on itself.

While in the hospital, Amanda discovered that Janet was her mother. Distraught, Amanda refused to have anything to do with Janet at first, but she eventually came around, as did Trevor, who now allowed Janet to be a parental figure for Amanda.

To the surprise of everyone including himself, Trevor began to fall in love with the woman he had long referred to as Janet from Another Planet. Tim, Trevor's stepson by Natalie, was not amused and began a reign of terror trying to break them up, including staging a fake kidnapping implicating Janet—who did have a history of such things—but his ruse was eventually discovered. When Trevor tried to propose, however, Janet turned him down because of a promise she had made to her sister, Natalie.

In order to convince Trevor she didn't love him, Janet hired an actor to pose as her ex-husband, Axel Green and arranged a fake wedding. Then Trevor uncovered her scheme and secretly arranged a real wedding. He confronted Janet, who confessed. After Natalie appeared, in spirit form, and absolved Janet of her past sins, Janet and Trevor were married.

Whether Janet will continue to walk the straight and narrow remains to be seen.

Of Special Note: Kate Collins originally played the dual role of Janet and Natalie.

Real-Life Soap Opera: Robin Mattson was born in Los Angeles. She knew from an early age that she wanted to act, and she began her career at the tender age of six. She made appearances on numerous television shows, including *Daniel Boone, The John Forsythe Show, Gentle Ben,* and *Flipper.*

As precocious as she was professionally, Robin was equally gifted academically, attending high school and college simultaneously via an advanced placement program. Though she majored in psychology, after her education was completed, Mattson returned to acting, guest-starring in television series such as *Charlie's Angels* and *Happy Days,* and appearing in television movies and feature films, including *Doctor's Private Lives* and *Return to Macon County.*

For the most part, Mattson's daytime characters have been of the dastardly variety, with the exception of her first serial part—a brief stint as Hope Bauer on *Guiding Light.* Next came a three-year run as the evil Heather Webber on *General Hospital.* Mattson had found her niche. For seven years, she starred as the scheming Gina Capwell on *Santa Barbara.* When that soap was canceled in 1993, Mattson suddenly found herself with unaccustomed time on her hands.

"I was so used to being busy," she recalls. She used the down time as an opportunity to follow up on another lifelong interest—cooking.

"I recognized the fact that I had always wanted to go to culinary school, so I would have knowledge to back enthusiasm. But school turned out to be much more grueling than daytime. Suddenly, I was learning about and being tested on rotating kitchen stock and pest control as well as how to hold a knife!"

Mattson became a student at the L.A. International Culinary Institute, taking a three-month curriculum called the Gastronomic Directives Course. Shortly after graduating, Mattson was offered the role of Janet on *All My Children*. She accepted but wasn't content to work only on the soap. Now she had a new desire—to combine her cooking skills with her television notoriety. The result was a flurry of celebrity chef appearances on talk shows, which led to her being hired to host the Lifetime cable network show *The Main Ingredient*. In addition, she became a national spokeswoman for PAM cooking spray and created her own line of food products, called Culinary Creations.

Mattson's goal on *The Main Ingredient* was to teach viewers about food and not just present recipes. She wanted people to see cooking as enjoyment, not tedium, because for her, food is a big part of socializing. "I love entertaining and getting together with friends and cooking, testing, talking, and eating."

Robin and her significant other, manager Henry Neuman, also collaborated on a cookbook, *Soap Opera Café*. "Neither one of us quite knew what we were getting into," Mattson admits. "It has really been an incredible project, a lot harder to put together than it appeared at first. We did a tremendous amount of cooking and testing, and spent a lot of time developing recipes."

One of the inspirations behind Robin's love of cooking was her late father, Paul Mattson. "My father was a chef, and he and I were very close," Robin says. "One Christmas he gave me his commercial cookware that he had used for years—big oversized pots and pans.

I love those. I still have them and I use them constantly, and I have his butcher block in my kitchen that he cooked on. So those are very, very treasured items that I really enjoy on a regular basis, and they bring back wonderful memories of my father."

Robin and Henry live in New York and continue to develop various projects, including more planned cookbooks.

Awards and Accolades: Mattson has been honored with four Emmy nominations and six *Soap Opera Digest* Awards—three for Best Comedic Performance and three for Best Villainess.

Trivia: Robin is the only actress to pick up *Soap Opera Digest* Awards for work on three different shows.

Div-o-Meter: 2—Although she can be a nasty piece of work onscreen, the humor Mattson brings to her characters offsets her criminal inclinations; and offcamera, Mattson is more apt to feed her peers than ruffle many feathers.

BEVERLEE McKINSEY

Beverlee McKinsey—Another World's
Iris and Guiding Light's *Alexandra*—
knows how to make an exit.

Crowning Role: Iris Carrington on *Another World* and *Texas*

Reign: 1972–81

Other Notable Roles: Martha Donnelly on *Love Is a Many Splendored Thing* (1970–71); Emma Ordway on *Another World* (1972); and Alexandra Spaulding on *Guiding Light* (1984–92)

Character's Most Notable Pursuit: Being simultaneously above-it-all snobbish and in-your-face meddlesome

Character's Occupations: Socialite and publishing executive

Character's Full Name: Iris Cory Carrington Delaney Bancroft Wheeler

Husbands: Eliot Carrington, Robert Delaney, Brian Bancroft, and Alex Wheeler

Character's Diva-lution: Iris first moseyed into Bay City in December 1972. Born in New York City, she was estranged from her mother, Sylvie Kosloff, but adored her father, Mac Cory, so naturally she despised Mac's new wife, Rachel. In her attempts to break them up, however, she merely succeeded in disappointing her father and making herself look bad.

When Mac died in 1989, Iris was devastated—a situation made worse by Rachel's involvement with Carl Hutchins, Mac's worst enemy.

Iris has been married four times. Her first husband was Eliot Carrington, who she married in the 1960s even though she knew she was carrying Alex Wheeler's child. She was in love with Alex, but Alex was poor, while Iris was very wealthy so . . . what's love got to do with it? When Dennis was born, she passed him off as Eliot's. Ironically, Eliot would later gain custody of Dennis while Iris spent her time being a socialite. Mac used his ample resources to reconcile the couple in 1973, although a year later, they split for good.

In 1976, Iris fell for designer Robert Delaney, and they were married. Less than a year later, however, Iris's deceptions destroyed the marriage. Just eight months later, she married again, this time to Brian Bancroft, in whom Iris had met her match. Because he saw himself in her, he was able to tolerate her behavior longer than most. That said, the marriage ended in 1980, shortly before Iris moved to Houston to be with her son. While in Texas, Iris married Alex, who was murdered by the mob a year later.

The character of Iris returned to *Another World* in 1988, shortly before her father's death. She left again in 1994 on her way to jail. On the day her father's widow was to marry his arch rival Carl Hutchins, Iris shot Carl with what she believed were blanks— intending only to scare him away from marrying Rachel. But unbeknownst to Iris, someone else with a vendetta against Rachel had put real bullets in the gun. Although Iris discovered the truth, she couldn't prove it. She was convicted of attempted murder and sent to state prison.

Of Special Note: After *Texas* was canceled and McKinsey joined *Guiding Light,* Carmen Duncan took over the role of Iris on *Another World* from October 1988 to September 1994. On *Texas,* Beverlee McKinsey became the first soap star to ever have sole star billing.

Real-Life Soap Opera: Beverlee McKinsey was born in McAlester, Oklahoma, on August 9, 1940, and began her professional career on a public broadcasting channel in Boston, hosting the children's show *The Make Believe Clubhouse.*

She made her soap opera debut on *Love Is a Many Splendored Thing,* where she met her future husband, Berkeley Harris. She first appeared on *Another World* in the small role of Emma Ordway, only to return later the same year as the formidable Iris Cory. In 1980, her extremely popular character was spun off into a new serial, *Texas.* Unfortunately, NBC scheduled *Texas* opposite *General Hospital* and not even Beverlee could overcome that juggernaut. She left the series after a year, and *Texas* was canceled not long after.

After taking some time away from daytime, McKinsey made a triumphant return to daytime as Alexandra Spaulding on *Guiding Light,* a part she played from 1984 to her abrupt departure in 1992. Since then, she has made only brief forays back to television, such as a six-day appearance as Myrna on *General Hospital* in 1994, a gig McKinsey says she took only because she "needed six days of work to qualify for my union medical insurance."

As for Myrna, McKinsey notes wryly, "She's quite different from anyone I had ever played before. Myrna used to be an actress and a dancer in clubs who wore skimpy costumes and played around a lot with wealthy men. Now she's a poor woman who's down on her luck—she owns a candy store."

Although there was hope among soap fans that her brief reemergence signaled a comeback, Beverlee, who is widowed, waved aside the speculation. "I'm loving my free time. I've always loved to read and I've never had any time to before. I have my little doggie; I've got sunshine and the ocean outside my front door. It's not a bad life."

Awards and Accolades: Nominated for four Emmys as Outstanding Actress, Beverlee was named Best Actress by *Afternoon TV* and was twice voted Favorite Villainess by *Soap Opera Digest.*

Most Notable Real-Life Diva Moment: Leaving for vacation and never coming back to work.

On August 5, 1992, McKinsey finished the day's taping of *Guiding Light* aware that it would be her last. As far as everyone else knew, Beverlee was leaving for a European vacation, but in fact, she had decided to quit the show for good. And she had the power to do just that. Her contract contained an out-clause that not even then–executive producer Jill Farren Phelps knew about, which allowed McKinsey to quit with only eight weeks notice, regardless of how major a storyline she might currently have. As it happened, August 5 was Beverlee's last day before a previously scheduled six-week vacation—and with the show two weeks ahead in filming, she could write her letter of resignation and never look back.

"I've had out-clauses in my contracts for years," Beverlee noted later. "Maybe they didn't read the contract. It's not my job to tell 'em what's in their contracts—and it's not my fault they're surprised. And they were to a degree. They didn't see this coming. I didn't see this coming. I didn't make the decision until July. Actually, I've been considering leaving soaps since 1978. That's the first time I quit daytime. I only had to work 14 more years to make it stick."

McKinsey gave only one farewell interview, to *TV Guide*'s Michael Logan, during which she discussed her unexpected departure that literally left *Guiding Light* reeling.

"It was time for me to go," she said simply. "This last year has been too difficult in terms of the hours that I've been asked to work. The hours got entirely too long. At first, I thought I'd ask them to cut me back—but you can't do that. I didn't want to anger my fellow actors. It affects all the other actors in your storyline, many of whom have been at *Guiding Light* longer than I have. Decreasing my story could mean decreasing theirs and [consequently] their workdays, their income. They have homes in the suburbs. They have families. You don't want to do that to your friends.

"So the more I thought about it, the solution was simply just to go! I'm burnt out and the only solution to that is to stop—and stop immediately."

"The show has been working me way too hard and the day finally came where I needed to exercise that clause. That, after all, is what it's there for. I no longer want to get up every morning at 4:45 and sit in a studio every night until 10. I want my life back. But I won't say anything bad about *Guiding Light*."

At the time, it was suspected that McKinsey would leave New York and move to the West Coast, where her son Scott, a television director, lived. She, however, put the kibosh to any idea of her joining any L.A.–based soap.

"I don't want to do a soap again," she told Logan candidly. "The only thing I'd like to do is a sitcom. Of course, I don't even have an agent! You know what I'm saying? I've worked for so long in daytime with no plans of ever doing anything else.

"I'm a big deal in daytime but nobody else gives a rat's hip about us soap people. And I think I'd only want to do a sitcom. I don't want to do guest shots. . . . I'd love it if Linda Bloodworth Thomason would just ring my phone—but I don't think that's gonna happen!

I'm not even in the Academy Player's Directory. If you wanted to find me, you wouldn't know how.

"So, you see, I really have no plans. I just know that I don't want to do *Guiding Light* anymore."

When asked whether she had realized the shockwaves she would cause by leaving, McKinsey seemed genuinely bemused.

"They're going around saying, 'She's irreplaceable.' What foolishness! Meryl Streep is irreplaceable. Everybody else you can replace. It's silly. I, myself, can think of ten women who can play Alexandra." *Guiding Light* did, indeed, replace McKinsey—with actress **Marj Dusay** (see pages 51–57).

In addition to feeling overworked, McKinsey admitted she was also unhappy with the unsympathetic direction the writers had taken Alexandra.

"What they've done with Alexandra during the last six months is close to assassination but I would have continued to play it if I'd been happy. That was not the straw that broke this camel's back. I've been doing daytime twenty-two years now. When you do it as long as I have, you go through a lot of periods where you don't like what they're writing for the characters. Or you don't like the person you're playing opposite. Or something, there's always something. But you're able to keep going for various reasons: One, you need the money and, two, you like the people you're working with, the family feeling you have there.

"But when you get tired, when you find that you just don't have a minute in the week that you can do anything but that show, then those things get bigger. When you're spending 12 or 13 hours a day there, those things suddenly get huge. When you're tired, you can't get past the other problems.

"This should be no secret to anybody. In 1978, I told Procter and Gamble I can put up with a lot. Bad writing. Bad acting. Bad working conditions. But when I'm tired, I get angry. And when I get angry, you don't want me around. I'm very professional. I behave really well. And I always do my work really well. But when I get tired and angry, I begin to behave in a way that is not me. I'm not proud of it and it shocks people."

As for why she kept her intentions from her castmates, Beverlee was all business.

"The next day, Vincent Irizarry said to somebody, 'My God, if I'd known those were her last scenes, I don't think I could have made it through.' And that is one of the reasons I didn't tell anyone, because that would have been wrong for the scenes. Nick doesn't feel about Alexandra the way Vince feels about Beverlee. It would have been wrong to see heartbreak on his face. We got the scenes in the can true to the story because absolutely nobody at that moment knew except me. They didn't take The Shot 'cause it's the last time we'll ever see Beverlee. No they just did what they would normally do.

"And when it was over, I said, 'That's the name 'o that tune, guys, I'm outta here.' I was able to say good-bye one-on-one to all the members of the crew and the actors that I feel close to. And those that I didn't encounter, I called them, but that's the way I wanted to do it. I didn't want weeks and weeks of people running through my dressing room and crying and going, 'Oh, my God, you've only got four more shows!' and 'Why are you doing this!? Oh, and by the way, could I have your shoes?' You know, that kinda crap.

"And I didn't want a surprise party with balloons and stale tacos and bad margaritas. I've been to sooo many of those at *Guiding Light*, I really didn't want one of those for me. I wanted to leave the way I came, without any fuss—just saying good-bye to the people I cared about on a one-to-one level without some Mexican band playing in the background. When people leave, we always go to Mexican restaurants and everyone gets drunk and says things they regret the next morning. No, no, I did not want to do another one of those."

Trivia: Another World is the only soap to have launched two spin-offs: *Somerset* (1970–76) and *Texas* (1980–82).

Div-o-Meter: 10—Forget the fact that McKinsey is truly one of the most talented and classiest grande dames of daytime, no one has ever made a more dramatic exit from a daytime career. Garbo would be very proud.

JULIET MILLS

While many soap characters have been called witches, Tabitha Lenox (Juliet Mills) actually is one!

Crowning Role: Tabitha Lenox on *Passions*

Reign: July 1999–present

What Juliet Says About Tabitha: "She is pretty bad, just a bad girl. Who knows what's in store for her. I reckon at some point there will be some comeuppance. Mercifully, all her evil schemes are not successful but she is just a marvelous character, even though she is a little wicked."

Character's Most Notable Pursuit: Turning creepy dolls into creepy children

Character's Diva-lution: Tabitha Lenox is one of those neighbors from our worst nightmares. Her seemingly sweet and thoughtful nature hides a dark side of evil.

Passions

Normally, the advent of a new soap is cause for excitement among daytime viewers, who hope against hope for the Next Big Thing. The reality, however, is that launching a truly successful soap is as difficult as launching the next *NYPD Blue*—it just doesn't happen that often. The last soap to make it in a big way was *The Bold and the Beautiful*—back in 1987.

With that kind of history going against it, it seems amazing that NBC would have saddled its newest soap, *Passions,* with the label The Show that Killed *Another World.* In a move that shocked fans and critics alike, NBC spared *Sunset Beach,* the lowest-rated daytime serial, and instead canceled the venerable *Another World* to make way for its new youth-oriented soap, creating a cadre of viewers already prepared to hate *Passions.*

Unfortunately, some critics hated it even more. *Entertainment Weekly* graded it an F+, saying:

"The astonishingly cretinous new soap opera *Passions* replaces the 35-year-old *Another World* and is apparently intended to represent the new wave in soaps. Among its touted innovations: A cast that is young, multicultural, and beautiful enough to give *Felicity* a run for its hair-gel budget (the graying soap genre needs to attract younger viewers); plus the addition of supernatural themes to the usual array of bad marriages and illicit affairs, in order to draw in . . . well, whom, exactly? Agoraphobes who post romantic Mulder-Scully fan fiction on *X-Files* websites?"

The reviewer saved his sharpest barbs for the character of Timmy, Tabitha's doll-child portrayed by Josh Evans, the diminutive actor who had a recurring role as a child prodigy attorney on *Ally McBeal*. "I am planning to take a short leave of absence to have surgically removed from my mind the image of Timmy, the mischievous doll created by Tabitha to wreak havoc in Harmony and cause nausea in viewers." Ouch. *Passions* is the brainchild of former *Days of Our Lives* writer James E. Reilly, who seems oblivious to all the bad things being said about his baby. "There are all sorts of things you would have tweaked one way or another, but overall, I'm thrilled," he told *TV Guide Online*. And as far as the F, he notes, "The last show *Entertainment Weekly* gave an F to, I believe, was *Providence,* so hello!"

The soap is set in Harmony, a picturesque New England town that, according to an NBC release, "hides its secrets and mysteries behind church steeples, picket fences, and manicured lawns."

The storyline revolves around four families—the wealthy and powerful Cranes; the Lopez-Fitzgeralds, a Hispanic family with secret ties to the Cranes; the Bennetts, whose matriarch, Grace, can't remember the first twenty years of her life; and the Russells.

Reilly maintains that despite its early low ratings, *Passions* will catch on. "My primary drive for all of my stories is what will entertain the audience. They're my boss. The audience determines what the story should be. I have to guess what they're going to like. And so far, in twenty years, it's proven that if I like it, I'm on the same wavelength."

Only time will tell if he's right.

Tabitha, who lives next door to the Bennett family, is really a witch, who for fun, brings a doll to life to keep her company and to assist her in her spells, plots, and all-around mischief, such as levitating her neighbor Grace Bennett and having her float through the window.

Favorite Storyline: "I think probably the one where my little 'accomplish' comes to life and I am no longer alone. When Timmy turns into a real person instead of a doll."

Of Special Note: Juliet is the author of the book *Mind, Body, Soul and Balance.*

Real-Life Soap Opera: Juliet Mills was literally born into the acting business, the daughter of revered British actor Sir John Mills, and the sister of former Disney moppet Hayley Mills. She made her professional debut at just eleven weeks old in the patriotic wartime film *In Which We Serve,* directed by Noel Coward, who was Juliet's godfather.

"They needed a baby, and I happened to be hanging around the set with my mother," Juliet explains, laughing. "So it's always been a part of my life, my family environment, and I love acting in all mediums. I enjoy theater, films, and television."

Although Mills enjoys working in all areas, she has amassed the most credits in theater and feature films. Her stage productions include *A Midsummer Night's Dream* and the Tony Award–nominated *Five Finger Exercise.* She has appeared in films such as *Avanti, Twice Around the Daffodils,* and, most recently, *The Other Sister* with Diane Keaton and Juliette Lewis.

What little television work she has done has been memorable. She starred as Phoebe Figalilly, the nanny of the title in *Nanny and the Professor* from 1970 to 1971, and also appeared in the award-winning 1974 miniseries *QB VII.*

Despite her distinguished career, Mills wasn't simply handed the role of Tabitha. "I did an audition for the part with 100 other people and they picked me," she says. Because of the youth-oriented aspects of the soap, Mills is probably the senior cast member in more ways than one. But she finds the soap opera experience unique and refreshing.

It is a very new experience and I am enjoying it very much," she says, noting how different soap acting is from film work. "There is less time, and more work! Doing one show a day, that is unthinkable in film. You wouldn't do more than 5 or 6 pages a day. We do 50 pages a day!

"It is very time consuming. We have been working 14 to 18 hours a day five days a week! And then on the weekends there are all those lines to learn for the next week. It's very hard work, and there is a lot of learning involved, but I'm getting better at it."

Originating a role in a debuting series also appealed to her. "It's very exciting to be at the beginning of something. And this is the beginning of a new show, and we are all starting together. So it is very wonderful to be a part of it."

When she's not working her witchy ways, Mills relaxes at her home in Sherman Oaks, California, with her husband, actor Maxwell Caulfield, and their two children, Sean and Melissa.

Awards and Accolades: Mills received an Emmy Award for Outstanding Single Performance by a Supporting Actress in a Drama Special for *QB VII,* and a Golden Globe Award for *Nanny and the Professor.*

Most Notable Real-Life Diva Moment: Marrying a man eighteen years her junior. Juliet Mills met her future husband, Maxwell Caulfield, in 1980, while rehearsing for a production of *The Elephant Man* in Palm Beach, Florida. And just to show that perhaps a little

Tabitha lives inside her, Mills believes their relationship began in another life.

"I'm convinced that we had past lives together—and not just one, either," Juliet says sincerely. "We were instantly such familiar friends, I couldn't believe that I hadn't always known him."

Ironically, even though their May–December marriage, with the woman being the senior partner, is not usual in our society, Mills says their relationship is actually very traditional. "He likes a woman to make his house pretty and be pretty for him and that's the way I like to be."

As they near their twentieth wedding anniversary, they have the last laugh on cynics who doubted the couple would last twenty months.

Div-o-Meter: 5—Although many divas are indeed witches, the opposite is not necessarily true.

ERIKA SLEZAK

Is this Viki Lord or one of her alternate personalities?

Crowning Role: Victoria Lord on *One Life to Live*

Reign: March 17, 1971–present

What Erika Says About Viki: "She's never been an uninteresting character."

Character's Most Notable Pursuit: Psychological stability and a consistent personality, as it were

Character's Full Name: Victoria Lord Riley Burke Riley Buchanan Buchanan Carpenter

Husbands: Roger Gordon (marriage not legal), Joe Riley, Steve Burke, Clint Buchanan, and Sloan Carpenter

Character's Diva-lution: Victoria Lord was born into a powerful, wealthy, and prestigious family in the city of Llanview. Her widowed father, Victor Lord, owned the newspaper, the *Banner*. Viki adored her father and seemingly had the world at her feet, except for one problem—Niki Smith, her split personality alter ego. This put a strain on her relationship with Joe Riley, a reporter with whom Viki had fallen in love. After she and Joe married in 1970 against her father's wishes, Viki underwent treatment for her disorder and believed she was cured. But tragedy struck when Joe's car went over a cliff and she believed him to be dead.

Viki's life seemed to be turning around when she fell in love with Steve Burke, an executive at the *Banner,* and they were married. But their happiness was abbreviated by the shocking return of Joe, who hadn't died in the car accident after all. They were remarried and in 1976, had a son, Kevin, who was kidnapped from his crib but was eventually rescued.

Just when her life seemed to be settling into some kind of normalcy, a new threat presented itself in the guise of Dorian Cramer, whom Viki viewed as nothing more than a shameless opportunist. Victor Lord thought otherwise and married Dorian, who was indeed only after his money. When Victor died, Dorian became rich. Viki was so resentful and bitter that she suspected Dorian of killing her father. Dorian later was tried and convicted, although it wasn't the last Viki or Llanview would see of her.

In 1979, Viki met Joe's friend Clint Buchanan and it was dislike at first sight. What Viki didn't know was that Joe was dying and he hoped that Clint would be there for Viki. After Joe succumbed to a brain tumor—leaving Viki the single mother of Kevin and baby Joey—Clint went to work at the *Banner,* where he found himself falling in love with Viki. But it was a one-sided affair—Viki had no interest at all in Clint. That is, until he rescued her from kidnappers.

Once the ice was broken, Viki let down her guard and fell in love with Clint. They were married, with Clint happily stepping in as Kevin and Joey's father.

When Viki discovered that she had a half-sister, Tina, from an affair her father had had with her close friend Irene Manning, the shock resulted in another personality split and the return of the slutty Niki Smith. Viki's psychological backslide caused her marriage to end. For a long period, Niki completely took over Viki's personality, pretending to be Viki so that she could stay the dominant personality. Clint, however, eventually forced Niki into the background by pretending to be romantically involved with Tina—the shock over which brought Viki back. She and Clint remarried and Viki gave birth to Jessica.

As if Viki didn't have enough to deal with, in 1987 she had a near death experience, during which she was reunited with Joe in heaven. He told her it wasn't her time to die, and she returned to earth. Then Clint was blinded by a gunshot and disappeared back in time to 1888. Viki traveled through time to find Clint, who was about to marry Viki's ancestor Ginny—who looked suspiciously just like Viki.

In 1989, Viki discovered that she had been hypnotized into forgetting that she'd given birth as a teen. Her search for her daughter, Megan Gordon, led her to Eterna, an underground city created by her father. Only a few years after they were reunited, Viki endured the loss of her child as Megan died of lupus.

In 1994, Viki met Sloan Carpenter, a writer interested in Victor Lord. Viki fell in love with Sloan and left Clint, unaware that Sloan was dying. When she found out, she married Sloan, only to be left a widow, yet again, a few months later. The trauma of losing Sloan, coupled with the discovery of yet another illegitimate half sibling, triggered Viki's most severe psychological fissure yet, resulting in the appearance of not only Niki, but five additional alternate personalities: Tommy, Jean, Princess, Tori, and Victor.

This time, the underlying cause of Viki's lifelong condition was finally revealed: As a child, she had been sexually abused by her beloved father, Victor.

"It's good to have the character back," Erika said at the time. "And I'm glad they finally addressed the reason for Victoria's multiple personalities, a story the writers built up to beautifully."

"Before, Viki's split personality was done well dramatically but not with psychological accuracy," explained writer Malone, who thoroughly researched what is properly called dissociative identity disorder. What he discovered was that the phenomenon is usually caused by childhood sexual abuse.

Slezak also carefully researched her role. A therapist dealing with the disorder allowed her to study therapy tapes of a patient. "It was extraordinary because the patient was a lovely, quiet, very sweet person," Erika noted. "But in the middle of the session, all these alters come out, which is stunning to see. I said it almost looks like bad acting because it is so broad. Actually, it's quite painful.

"In multiples, they create all different sides of personalities to cope with their unbearable feelings. It's a very logical disorder."

Viki's identities each represented a different side of Viki's personality. Fourteen-year-old Tommy was rage; Jean was a cool, collected woman who protected Viki from harm; Princess was a six year old who relived her father's abuse and represented the child Viki was when the abuse started; Niki, the original alter, was created to enjoy sex; Tori wanted to tell the secret; and Victor represented her father. And in a surprising turn of events, it was revealed that Tori killed Viki's father as payback for the abuse.

After intensive therapy—and two Emmys for Slezak—Viki is finally believed to be cured. But is she really? With the worst seemingly behind her, Viki is now the full-time publisher of the *Banner* and one of Llanview's grandest dames.

Real-Life Soap Opera: Acting is literally in Erika Slezak's blood. She is the second of three children born to actor Walter Slezak and his wife, Johanna. Erika's grandfather was an operatic tenor, Leo Slezak, who sang in Vienna and Berlin as well as at the New Metropolitan Opera. Erika grew up in Hollywood until the family moved to New York City in 1954 after Walter was cast in the Broadway musical *Fanny,* for which he won a Tony Award.

Young Erika was obsessed with acting. "Except for about twenty minutes when I wanted to be a nun, it never occurred to me to do anything else," she says. "I wanted to be a serious actress in the worst possible way. When I was a sophomore in high school, my father talked to me about training for a career in acting. One thing my father did for me was not discourage my ambitions. But he made sure I had no illusions about the acting profession, explaining that it was going to be harder for me because I had a famous father. I would have to prove myself more than others and, as usual, he was right."

After graduating from the Convent of the Sacred Heart High School in Greenwich, Connecticut, Erika was accepted at London's Royal Academy of Dramatic Art. At seventeen, she was one of the youngest students ever granted admission. When she completed her studies, she returned to the United States and found work in regional theater, making $108 a week at the Milwaukee Repertory Theater.

In 1968, when she was only twenty-one, Slezak got married. It was a mistake. "He was a nice man," Erika says of her first husband. "But we had totally different ambitions." The married ended after three years.

She left Milwaukee in 1969 and continued working in theater, amassing credits including Sophocles' *Electra, The Philadelphia Story, The Skin of Our Teeth, Design for Living, Hedda Gabler, The Big Night, Othello, Mary Stuart, The Importance of Being Earnest, A Streetcar Named Desire, Barefoot in the Park, Music Man, Mr. Roberts, Tartuffe,* and *Blithe Spirit.*

Before leaving New York to play Desdemona in a Buffalo production of *Othello,* Slezak auditioned for *One Life to Live.* To her amazement, she got the job. "It happened so fast," Slezak recalls, noting that other than the character's name, she knew nothing about the part. "All I knew was that they were going to pay me for two years.

"God bless certain people who literally took me by the hand and led me through that first day because I had never done TV."

When that contract was up, she signed up again. "The character was so fun I said, 'Yeah, I'll do another two years.'"

That was twenty-eight years ago, which Erika admits is "shockingly long. I've been there more than half my life."

Slezak's private life has been considerably less traumatic than Viki's. She met her husband, Brian Davies, when they worked together in *The Circle* at Manhattan's Roundabout Theatre. Erika and Brian have two children, Michael, born in 1980, and Amanda Elizabeth, born in 1981. The family lives in Long Island, but the bright lights of Broadway already beckon to Amanda, who yearns to be an actress just like her mother. Although Slezak's father encouraged her dreams, she has mixed feelings about her own daughter's career goals. She has told her, "Don't do it because you think you want to be famous. Just do it because you love to act. Then the fame doesn't matter."

Slezak follows her own advice. Unlike so many other daytime actors who feel stifled by being labeled "soap" stars, Erika never felt the need to try to conquer primetime or film.

"I'm an actress because I love to act. OK, I'm not up on the big silver screen," she acknowledges. "But I play this real interesting character on television. Daytime is not afraid to tackle any story. Why should I leave this show and go and do nothing? People are dying to get into daytime because it's steady work. And," she adds, "just because I'm a success in daytime doesn't mean I'd be a success in nighttime or film."

That said, Slezak admits to having enjoyed filming a role in the primetime TV movie *Danielle Steel's Full Circle*. "It was terrific fun. And the kids thought it was cool because I had my own trailer."

More than anything, it seems that quality of life is what Slezak holds most dear, pointing out that being on daytime "enabled me to have a lifestyle I enjoy." A lifestyle that includes steady work and the freedom to be home in time to have dinner with her family.

Awards and Accolades: Erika Slezak has been honored with a record five Emmy Awards for Outstanding Actress—1984, 1986, 1992, 1995, and 1996.

Most Notable Real-Life Diva Moment: During an interview, Slezak showed the reporter one of her five Emmy Awards. "Look at this," the reporter described her as saying dismissively. "Detachable nameplates for the base. This one actually has double-stick tape on it."

Historical Footnote: Slezak might be best remembered as the woman who kept making Susan Lucci the perennial Emmy bridesmaid, besting her every year they went head to head. Because of all the hoopla surrounding Lucci's eighteen-year losing streak, *One Life to Live* producer Robyn Goodman felt Slezak's unprecedented fifth daytime Emmy was unfairly "obscured by everyone feeling badly for Susan. I understand that, but you don't want to neglect the person who was rewarded."

Trivia: In 1985, Donna Rice, the woman who torpedoed Gary Hart's presidential campaign, appeared as one of Niki Smith's friends, Jeannie.

Div-o-Meter: 6—Despite her longevity and the mantel full of Emmys, she's less a regal presence than a comforting earth mother.

© ROGER KARNBAD/
CELEBRITY PHOTO AGENCY, INC.

LOUISE SOREL

Louise Sorel plays Vivian Alamain, one of the nastiest pieces of work in daytime

Crowning Role: Vivian Alamain on *Days of Our Lives*

Reign: 1992–2000

Other Notable Roles: Augusta Lockridge on *Santa Barbara* (1984–86, 1988–89, 1990–91) and Judith Sanders on *One Life to Live* (1986–87)

What Louise Says About Vivian: "Vivian is more than off the wall; she's off the floor and off the ceiling. I don't feel I'm playing a villain; I'm playing a woman who's just determined to get what she wants. She's conniving, stubborn, selfish, flamboyant, manic, childish, strong, seductive, vindictive—all underlaid with a core of evil humor. It's a very funny role when you come right down to it."

Character's Most Notable Pursuit: Piling up the body count

Character's Occupation: Publishing executive

Character's Full Name: Vivian Alamain Kiriakis Jones DiMera

Husbands: Victor Kiriakis, Steven "Jonesy" Jones, and Stefano DiMera

Character's Diva-lution: Vivian Alamain breezed into Salem in March 1992, throwing a masquerade ball as her coming out party, as it were. It wasn't mere frivolity, however, that prompted Vivian's largesse. Her intent was to re-create an event from eight years earlier during which a notorious thief named Romulus made off with a fortune in jewels.

Salem's own amnesiac, John Black, thought he might be Romulus, but he was mistaken. Vivian's interest with Black didn't end there. At her urging, Vivian's nephew Lawrence agreed to exhume the grave of his brother Forrest, who had died as a child. To the surprise of nobody who's at all familiar with the goings-on in Salem, the casket was minus a corpse. A few DNA tests later and it was proved that John Black was really Forrest Alamain. The family reunion, however, was short-lived—as soon as his identity was verified, John/Forrest staked his share of the family inheritance. Vivian was not amused and swore to avenge his greed.

Vivian was always finding herself in the middle of trouble. When her foster son, Nicky, arrived in Salem, Vivian was the object of a blackmail attempt by a shyster lawyer who knew the truth of Nicky's parentage. When Nicky confronted the lawyer, a tussle ensued during which Nicky shoved the lawyer, causing her to hit her head and die.

In order to protect Nicky, Vivian and Lawrence took the lawyer's body and staged a car accident so the body would be incinerated amid the wreckage. When her nephew turned on her, however, Vivian was so upset she had a heart attack. Lawrence later discovered that

Nicky was really his and Carly's son. Desperate to keep Nicky for herself, Vivian plotted to kill Carly.

Then, when she was diagnosed with a fatal heart ailment, Vivian changed her mind—because she was going to die anyway, she thought she would frame Carly for her own murder. At a party, Vivian led Carly to a balcony, where she goaded her into an argument. Then Vivian intentionally fell over the balcony, intending to kill herself while making it look like Carly pushed her. Unfortunately for Vivian, Carly—a doctor—saved her life in surgery.

Suffering from the after-effects of her fall, Vivian became a self-appointed angel of death. While faking a coma, she began killing Carly's patients with cleaning fluid, hoping to frame her for those murders. When Carly caught Vivian in the act and tried to intervene, Vivian injected her with morphine. Afterward, she dosed Carly with drugs that made her appear to be dead. Aware that Carly was merely in a very deep state of unconsciousness, Vivian put a monitor in Carly's casket so that she could taunt her when Carly woke to find herself buried alive. Once Vivian recovered, however, she confessed. Carly was rescued and Vivian was institutionalized.

Vivian was not enamored with mental hospital living and began sneaking out. Of course she got caught. It was decided the only way to control Vivian was to lobotomize her. Just as she was to undergo the procedure, a fire fortuitously broke out, and her devoted employee, Ivan, rescued her.

After she had recovered, Vivian was at it again. Her plot this time was to win the affections of Victor Kiriakis. She went about it in a unique manner—she stole Victor and Kate's embryo and had herself artificially inseminated with it. (Don't ask.) After this trick, she got Victor to marry her, although he wasn't aware of it. (Really, don't ask.)

In an attempt to keep Kate from filling Victor in on Vivian's misdeeds, Vivian drugged Kate's coffee. The spiked java, however, was consumed by the pilot of Kate's plane, causing him to crash the aircraft. Of course, Kate's body was never found.

The following year, when Kate reappeared, Vivian revealed that not only was she Victor's wife but that she was about to give birth to his child—no small irony, considering they had never made love. After, Vivian told Victor that if he tried to divorce her, she'd file for custody of baby Phillip. It was all too much for Victor, who promptly had a stroke. And they divorced anyway.

Vivian next married Jonesy for financial security. What she didn't know was that Jonesy was in cahoots with Stefano, who was using Jonesy as a front, and that the money came from ill-gotten gain. After Jonesy's death, Vivian inherited his money—which was really Stefano's. In order to regain control of his wealth, Stefano controlled Vivian through a device implanted in her teeth, then married her.

When she found out what Stefano had done, Vivian vowed to get her revenge.

Of Special Note: In 1985, Sorel's *Santa Barbara* character, Augusta Lockridge, went temporarily blind. Sorel received a get-well card from President and Mrs. Reagan. Apparently, someone forgot to tell Reagan it was just a story.

Real-Life Soap Opera: Louise Sorel, known as Lou Lou to her friends, was born in Los Angeles. Her mother was a painter and pianist and her father the noted film producer Albert H. Cohen.

Louise attended Hollywood High and Los Angeles City College and was very active in their respective drama departments. She later received a two-year scholarship to the Neighborhood Playhouse in New York and made her Broadway debut a couple of years later in *Take Her, She's Mine,* opposite Art Carney and Elizabeth Ashley.

Her first film was *The Party's Over,* starring Oliver Reed and Eddie Albert. The movie was shot in London, and Louise began spending her weekends off in Paris, a short plane ride away. The experience made an indelible mark on Sorel, who embarked on a lifelong love affair with travel in general and Paris in particular.

Back in New York, Louise auditioned for a television pilot developed by Woody Allen called *The Laugh Makers,* alongside Alan Alda, David Burns, and Michael J. Pollard. "I was young and didn't really know what I was doing," she recalls, "and just did something silly. Poor Woody—he just stared at me and looked miserable, like I had ruined his day. I was shocked a few days later when I was told the role was mine."

The pilot didn't sell but Louise found ample work on Broadway, including a role in the George C. Scott vehicle *The Lion in Winter.* After Sorel married actor Herb Edelman, she began spending part of the year in Los Angeles and quickly amassed numerous guest-starring appearances, including *Medical Center, Big Valley, Ironside, Star Trek,* and *Night Gallery.* She also costarred in the steamy primetime series *The Survivors* with Lana Turner, George Hamilton, Kevin McCarthy, and Jan-Michael Vincent.

After she and Edelman divorced, Louise drifted back to stage work. While starring in *Volpone,* Sorel met and fell in love with her costar, Ken Howard (of TV's *The White Shadow* and *The Colbys*), but their subsequent marriage ended after only three years.

Now based in Los Angeles, Sorel resumed her television and film work. Because she was working steadily, Louise wasn't sure she wanted to accept the offer to play the flashy Augusta Lockridge on the then-new soap, *Santa Barbara.* Although she loved acting, soap operas were, to coin a phrase, another world.

"It's a ridiculous medium for an actor," comments Sorel. "I usually leave home for the studio at seven in the morning and don't get home until seven in the evening. We do an hour show every day, which would take eight days for a nighttime hour. You don't have much time to think about the various ways you might play a scene—you just have to wing it."

She obviously got the hang of it. When Augusta's storyline faded, Sorel moved back to New York to join *One Life to Live* as Judith Sanders. After a brief return to *Santa Barbara,* Sorel joined *Days of Our Lives* as Vivian Alamain, one of the nastiest pieces of work in daytime. Even so, Sorel doesn't view Vivian the way most others do.

"I don't like to be slotted because to me she's a woman who can do villainous things, but nobody thinks of themselves as a villainess. Vivian gets to do anything she wants and doesn't ever really pay for it. She gets about 30 minutes of hand-slapping when she does things, and then she goes on about her business. Who doesn't dream of a life like that?"

Louise has admitted having a hard time accepting some of the things the writers come up with. "I do balk at a lot. Believe me I do. And then I say 'Okay, you have a choice here. You can leave'—which has crossed my mind—'or you can just go and do it with the best possible style and commitment you can.'"

Despite Vivian's popularity, the character was written off the show in early 2000—partly because the show wanted to focus on younger characters. Sorel was anxious to return to stage work in New York. "I thrive better there. Every time I come back to New York, I fall in love with something new. I recently walked over the Brooklyn Bridge, which I had never done. It was so romantic—I was enthralled. "There are things about Los Angeles that are definitely plusses, but in the long run I think I'm a happier, healthier person in New York."

Awards and Accolades: Sorel has a mantelful of *Soap Opera Digest* Awards, including Outstanding Villainess, Outstanding Female

Scene Stealer, Outstanding Female Show Stopper, and Outstanding Supporting Actress. She was also named daytime television's Best Psychopath in a *TV Guide* reader's poll.

Causes: Vivian is very active with the Children's Cancer Foundation, the Celebrity Action Counsel for Women's Rehabilitation, and, she adds, "just about every animal protection group on the planet."

Most Notable Real-Life Diva Moment: Jetting off to Paris for a relaxing lunch.

Div-o-Meter: 7—Though Sorel refers to herself as "a real handful," the fact that she acknowledges that automatically brings her down to earth.

ROBIN STRASSER

Robin Strasser doesn't mind being called "high maintenance."

Crowning Role: Dorian Lord on *One Life to Live*

Reign: 1979–87, 1993–present

Other Notable Roles: Rachel Davis on *Another World* (1967–72) and Christina Karras on *All My Children* (1976–79)

Character's Most Notable Pursuit: Being the bane of Viki Lord's life

Character's Occupations: Doctor, ambassador, newspaper publisher, and businesswoman

Character's Full Name: Dorian Cramer Lord Callison Vickers Hayes

Husbands: Victor Lord, Herb Callison, David Vickers, and Mel Hayes

Character's Diva-lution: Dr. Dorian Cramer moved to Llanview in 1973, along with her mentally disturbed sister, Melinda, who had never recovered emotionally from an accident that destroyed her once-promising career as a pianist. In 1974, Dorian lost her license to practice medicine after she accidentally gave a patient an overdose. Dorian was so embittered by the loss of her career, she vowed to forever pay back the entire population of Llanview.

Dorian's first husband was the ailing Victor Lord, who was bedridden with a bad heart. Although she tended to him, she was far more interested in finance than romance. Luckily for her, shortly after she convinced him to name her his beneficiary, he was killed, leaving Dorian the mistress of Llanfair.

Because Victor's will stipulated that his estate would revert to his daughter, Viki, should Dorian ever remarry, Dorian was evicted from the house upon her marriage to Herb Callison, who Dorian believed would be elected governor. He was, but had to resign after it was discovered that Dorian had bought the election.

In 1981, Dorian's daughter Cassie—whose father, David Renaldi, was Dorian's lover in medical school—moved to Llanview. After Herb legally adopted Cassie, Renaldi showed up in town. When Dorian tried to get back together with David, Herb finally divorced her.

In 1986, Dorian was convicted of murdering a drug-dealing cultist, Mitch Laurence. She spent time in prison for the crime but was released when videotape surfaced that proved she had killed him in self-defense. Needing a break from life in Llanview, Dorian left to be an ambassador to the country of Mendorra.

She returned two years later for the sole purpose of destroying Viki Lord. Dorian's vendetta against Viki was put on hold after Dorian was diagnosed with breast cancer, but once in remission, she was back with a vengeance.

Much of their antagonism stemmed from Viki's belief that Dorian had murdered Victor. In fact, many years later, Dorian was convicted of the crime and was sent to death row. However, Dorian was spared when David Vickers arrived in Llanview. Not only did he claim—falsely as it would turn out—to be Victor Lord's long lost son, but he also produced a phony diary that cleared Dorian. Dorian really was innocent, and it was later revealed that it was actually one of Viki's multiple personalities that had killed Victor. After a run-in with one of Viki's other personalities, Dorian married David Vickers and laid low for a while.

She resurfaced when she divorced David and met newspaper reporter Mel Hayes, who relocated from Washington, D.C., to be with Dorian. Did we mention he was an alcoholic? Suspicious that Dorian was hiding a secret, Mel investigated her past and discovered that as a child Dorian had witnessed her mother kill her father. To put closure to her childhood trauma, Dorian tracked down her mother, Sonya, who was living in Ohio—and completely insane. When Sonya went murderously berserk, Dorian killed her.

After surviving that ordeal, Dorian almost lost her life when she was shot during a holdup at a Llanview store. As she fought for her life, Dorian's spirit traveled to Hell and back and when she came to, she vowed to change her ways and be a better person. She married Mel and tried to make amends with Viki. However, a front-burner storyline in 1999 had Dorian accidentally running down Viki's pregnant daughter, Jessica, killing the baby Jessica was carrying—thereby propelling the feud to new heights.

Of Special Note: The role of Dorian has also been played by Nancy Pinkerton (1973–77), Claire Malis (1977–79), and Elaine Princi (1989–93).

Real-Life Soap Opera: Robin Strasser was born in the Bronx and raised in Manhattan. After graduating from the famed High School of Performing Arts, she attended the Yale School of Drama on a full scholarship.

She recalls, "When I needed money, I would work at dress stores or sportswear stores. One of them was Henri Bendel's. I was such a good salesgirl they were ready to train me as a junior assistant buyer."

Strasser wasn't interested in pursuing any career other than acting, especially acting in the theater. And despite her heavy soap schedule, Strasser has continued to appear in plays, including the Broadway production of Michael Cristofer's Pulitzer Prize–winning *The Shadow Box* and Neil Simon's *Chapter Two.* Robin is also a founding member of the American Conservatory Theatre and has worked with such prestigious theatrical companies as the Williamstown Theatre Festival and Los Angeles's Mark Taper Forum.

Nor is she a stranger to primetime, having guest-starred in series such as *Murphy Brown, Dear John, China Beach, The Young Riders, Highway to Heaven, Civil Wars,* and *Murder, She Wrote.* She also had recurring roles on *Knot's Landing* and *Coach.*

Strasser's first daytime role was on *Another World,* playing Rachel Davis, who Robin describes as someone who "had to make it. She had to be successful. She was a girl from the wrong side of the tracks. She just wanted the good life."

After leaving that soap, Robin spent the next two-and-a-half years in Los Angeles. Now the mother of two sons, Nicholas and Benjamin, she was approached by ABC to take over the role of Cathy on *One Life to Live,* a character who had just stolen a baby. She turned the role down, telling the network she didn't want to return to daytime as "a replacement."

Instead, she joined *All My Children* as a new character, Dr. Christina Karras, in 1976. Unfortunately, it wasn't a match made in daytime heaven. "I said to ABC I didn't want to continue, that the part and I did not mesh," revealed Strasser. "One of the first things I did when I came on the show was tell a character that her newborn baby was retarded, had brain damage, and should be put in a home. And I did not want to play a character that would say such a thing. And they made me say it."

Strasser notes that she knew this was not a character she would want to play for years. "If you don't adopt and marry and take into your very heart and soul the character you are playing on a soap, you are probably only going to be doing the role for six weeks, six months, but you are never going to make it to the six-year mark. You have to love and adopt and own and defend and adore your character, whether it is a bad guy or a good guy."

After making her feelings known, Strasser was called in to a meeting with Jackie Smith, the head of daytime programming at the time. "She had this impression that I didn't like this character because she wasn't a good person. 'No,' I said, 'I love playing bad guys. Did you ever see me on *Another World?*' She hadn't."

Smith offered Strasser the chance to take over the role of Dorian on *One Life to Live*. Robin would later let loose with her opinion of how Dorian could be improved. Her first suggestion was to increase Dorian's style and humor quotient. She wanted to "give the audience a glimpse of what people love to see rich people do . . . live excessively. And I added she should dress marvelously and flamboyantly, that there should be some campy humor when she screws up. Then maybe she can be around for two to five years."

What nobody at the network realized is that Strasser was actually desperate for the job. As she explains, "I was on the verge of a divorce and needed a job badly."

So, when the show's director mentioned that Strasser had a reputation of being difficult to work with, she burst into tears. "We all have these buttons—and I am not a person who cries easily—but it went straight to my deepest center and I bawled.

"He had thought I would defend myself or get angry and want to know the source, but instead my feelings were so hurt. I was so misunderstood that I just sobbed. You know, you can't be on a very good show and tell them that your character is gray and that you are leaving and be in the middle of a marriage that is disintegrating and look like the cheeriest camper of the summer."

As to the perception that she's difficult, Strasser is reflective. "There are an awful lot of people who have that issue around their name—'She's difficult' or the new phrase that makes it easier to say is 'high maintenance.'

"But high maintenance can also refer to cars you collect, fine wine you want to store, antiques you want to preserve—you wouldn't apply a quick coat of Mop and Glo to a fine oak floor . . . so I'm okay about that.

"I hope that in the end people can see that I do care. What I don't do anymore is fight with anybody. . . . I have had my battles. I am not going to betray myself or the audience whom I value. But I will walk away rather than be in a toxic situation. I will wave a white flag. I will shake hands. I will not burn a bridge."

In the end, Strasser was cast as Dorian and switched soaps literally overnight, giving her no time to familiarize herself with the storyline or characters. "I had so many names to sort out and by the end of the first day I was exhausted but I got through it."

As she sat on a couch regrouping, Strasser says Erika Slezak, who plays Dorian's mortal enemy, Viki, plopped down beside her.

"She said, 'You are going to be very good in this part. And I am very glad you have joined the cast.' That was terribly classy of her. I really needed that. There is a certain kind of real grace that some people are lucky to have and it has a lot to do with Erika's upbringing and fine family tradition."

Not one to sit at home when not working, Strasser's varied interests include hiking, cooking, and home renovation. She is also a certified Kripalu Yoga teacher and leads workshops on yoga as support for mid-life transition. She says if she has one overriding philosophy, it is: "Be realistic, but don't give up your dream. I am on the tenacious side. I admire those people who have a way of following a dream where they don't need the validation of other people."

Awards and Accolades: Strasser has won an Emmy Award for Outstanding Actress (1992), a *Soap Opera Digest* Award as Outstanding Actress (1996), and a *Soap Opera Update* Award for Best Actress (1996).

Causes: Bringing the issue of menopause out into the open. Annoyed at how menopause seemed to be a dirty word, Strasser was one of the first celebrities to publicly discuss her personal experiences.

"*Menopause* is like the last tasteless word left," she says. "Is it because it labels us as having passed a certain era? Do we lose value in the marketplace? Any risk to my career or my allure is far outweighed by the fact that I really feel attention should be paid to the issue and more medical research should be done. I want to share with the many women who are going through some uncomfortable times that they are not alone and that there is help.

"Menopause is an ignored time in a woman's life," continues Strasser. "But I perceive it as a health issue. The topic has laid dormant for so long but the importance of it is only going to grow greater as we reach the year 2000, as an enormous amount of women from the baby-boom generation reach that stage in their life."

Strasser has been candid about the effects menopause had on her life and career, and how at first she was ignorant about what was happening to her.

"There was depression and severe mood swings, which were huge and hard to live with. And I had short-term memory loss, which is really bad for a soap opera actress. We often have fifty pages of dialogue to memorize a day. I really thought I was having a nervous breakdown."

Strasser finally understood what was happening after she had an estrogen level test and began taking hormone supplements. She also became diet conscious and started studying yoga. Now she says, "I've never felt better in my life."

Although it can be unnerving at first, Strasser believes menopause can be empowering because it forces women to take charge of their own health. "The answer to being scared about menopause is to be as informed as possible."

Strasser is also active in fundraising for AIDS research, the New York City Blood Center, and Telicare. In addition, she is on the Advisory Board of the American Menopause Foundation and is a spokesperson for the National Osteoporosis Foundation.

Most Notable Real-Life Diva Moment: Finally meeting her long lost half-sister.

"I was doing a play in Los Angeles," Strasser recalls, "and without any prior notification, between the matinee and evening performance, the stage doorman called upstairs and said, 'Robin, there is a young lady here and she says she is your sister.' I said, 'In my family, anything is possible,' and I had heard that I did have a half-sister somewhere.

When Strasser opened the door and came face to face with her sister, she says it was like "looking in a mirror. We look that much alike. And we just fell into each other's arms and started crying. We stay in touch through phone calls now."

Strasser also has a half-brother, all sharing the same father.

Trivia: Who was the other diva rumored to be Robin Strasser's sister? None other than Susan Lucci. For several years this rumor refused to die, and at one point it was embellished to where Phyllis Diller was said to be Susan and Robin's mother. "Phyllis made jokes about it in her comedy act," Robin says. "I always thought it would be great for all of us to do a charity fund-raiser someday."

Div-o-Meter: 9—Although equally edgy and tough onscreen and off, Strasser lacks the intangible grand flair necessary to top the chart.

ANNA STUART

Far from the model mother, Another World's *Donna Love ran her own daughter down with a car.*

Crowning Role: Donna Love on *Another World*

Reign: January 1983–November 1986; February 1989–June 1999

Other Notable Roles: Toni Ferra Powers on *The Doctors* (1971–77); Dr. Gina Dante on *General Hospital* (1977–78)

What Anna Says About Donna: "She loved her family, fiercely. And she loved. She had lots of judgments and lots of restrictions about her, but there was a bigness in her that she allowed to happen. Matt brought that out in her, Jake brought that out in her, but there was a tiger there. I think she was a truly good person."

As *Another World* neared the end of its run, Stuart mused over what she would like to do if she had the chance to bring Donna back on another soap: "I would like to explore Donna's strength and savvy in a more productive way, meaning for her not to be such a pain in the neck and be such a helpless, stupid female. I'd like to find out that she's a real sharp cookie, to have Donna learn something and actually not be so much of a buffoon as she has been. Could I be projecting? I mean, after all, we are our characters."

Character's Most Notable Pursuit: Staying out of jail

Character's Full Name: Donna Love Hutchins Hudson Hudson Cory.

She married her second husband, Michael Hudson, in 1986. The couple renewed their vows in 1987, were divorced in January 1988, remarried eleven months later, and finally divorced for good in 1991. Her marriage to Matthew Cory was annulled after three months.

Character's Diva-lution: For more than a decade, in two different stints, Stuart has played socialite Donna Love, who seems to have a penchant for spending time in jail for crimes she didn't commit—while eluding punishment for those she did.

Born in Bay City, Donna met the love of her life, Michael Hudson, when he was hired as a stable boy at the Love estate. They became lovers when Donna was just sixteen. In one of her more foolish acts, Donna tried to get Michael jealous by flirting with his brother, John. But Donna lost control of the situation and was raped by John in the back seat of his car. Ashamed and frightened, Donna never told anyone about the assault.

Her relationship with Michael came to an abrupt end after her father, Reginald Love, found out about the affair. He roughed Michael up and ran him out of town, saying Donna never wanted to see him again. What Michael didn't know was that Donna was pregnant. She later gave birth to twins, Victoria and Marley. Reginald forced Donna to give Victoria up for adoption and passed Marley off as Donna's sister.

Donna was briefly married in the 1970s to Carl Hutchins; the union was seldom talked about, until he came back into Donna's life in 1984, threatening to reveal the secret about Marley's birth. In 1985, Victoria arrived in Bay City, intent on stealing the Love family fortune. She had discovered the truth of her parentage when she was eighteen and felt abandoned and betrayed by her mother. Initially, Victoria hated Marley, but after Marley contracted a mysterious disease generic to daytime dramas, she and Donna were reunited with Victoria.

In 1986, Michael Hudson returned to Bay City as a self-made millionaire. He rekindled his romance with Donna and they were married. When he found out he was a father, he was anxious to establish a relationship with the twins. That same year, however, Donna suffered a nervous breakdown after her father showed her a photograph of John holding the newborn twins, apparently confirming her deepest fear—that John was actually the girls' father.

When John returned to Bay City in 1987, Donna found herself physically attracted to him but refused to acknowledge it. When John finally managed to get Donna primed for seduction, though, he couldn't go through with it, out of respect for his brother. Instead, he and Donna vowed to just be friends. Unfortunately for them, they were in bed when they came to this conclusion and were seen in this compromising position by the ever-conniving Victoria Hudson. As a result, Michael found out and, wrongly believing Donna and John were having an affair, filed for divorce.

In the ensuing years, Donna would spend more time in court than most attorneys. In July 1990, Toby and Eve Miller sued to regain custody of the son they had given up to Donna and Michael for adoption. When the Millers' lawyer threatened to reveal Donna's affair with Jake McKinnon, Donna gave up all custody rights to Mikey, who was then returned to his natural parents.

A year later, Donna's daughter Marley was on trial for the attempted murder of Jake McKinnon, Donna's former lover and the object of both Victoria and Marley's desire. In a spurt of parental selflessness, Donna dramatically told the packed courtroom that she was the murderer and was immediately put in the pokey. Naturally, once the police investigated her claim, they realized she had been lying to protect her daughter. Donna was released.

Donna managed to stay out of legal trouble for a while after that and instead found love with a much younger man, Matthew Cory. Their romance brought to the fore all sorts of issues regarding aging and the nature of love. "I think my thing with Matthew, the menopause scare that I had, is about as real as you can get on that level," Anna notes.

Donna and Matthew initially got to know each other as business partners in late 1992, as co-owners of Bay City's local television station, KBAY. (Despite her penchant for getting arrested, Donna Love was a rather savvy businesswoman. In addition to KBAY, she once owned Bay City General Hospital, and in 1997 she bought the Harbor Club.) Their relationship took a turn during the time Donna went undercover as a prostitute in order to expose corrupt politicians for one of the station's shows. The more Matthew exhibited concern for her, the more attracted Donna was to him. But she couldn't get past their age difference and the fact she could literally be his mother. But Matthew persisted and finally, during a raging snowstorm, they made love in the KBAY news van.

In 1994, despite her initial concerns, Donna agreed to marry Matthew. Their marriage kept getting postponed, however, mostly because of Donna's lingering doubts. In November 1995, Matthew insisted they elope. Donna agreed. Before leaving, she went to see Michael Hudson to get back some cufflinks that had been her wedding present to him. While they talked, their favorite song began to play on the radio, and caught up in the moment, they made love.

Donna assumed this meant she and Michael would get back together and was crushed when he told her he had no such intentions. He wasn't the person she needed. Crushed, Donna ran back to Matthew, who had no idea she had been ready to dump him, and they were married.

Shortly before Christmas, Matthew learned of Donna's betrayal and asked that their marriage be annulled. Donna tried to win Matthew back. During this time, Matthew became a suspect in the Bay City Stalker murders. One would think that having already spent time in jail, Donna would watch herself around police types, but when detectives questioned Matthew, Donna flipped out to the point that she became a suspect herself. The real killer took advantage of this and began planting evidence to make Donna look guilty. Once again she was arrested and spent time in prison before being proved innocent.

Once the murders were solved and Donna was free, she told Matthew that she was responsible for the failure of their relationship and she still hoped they could be friends. He agreed, although it was clear he still regretted they weren't together.

Donna's tumultuous relationship with her twin daughters reached its nadir in 1998, when Donna ran down Marley with her car, believing she was Victoria. By the time the truth came out, Marley was so bent on winning her ex-husband Jake back from Victoria that she kidnapped her sister and pushed her mother down a flight of stairs. Donna was confined to a wheelchair, having been rendered partially paralyzed by the fall. "She did indeed have an injury," explains Stuart, "but I think in terms of the psychological trauma, let's get real: When you look at what she'd been through at that point, with her husband dying and her daughter getting hit by the car she was driving . . . I think it was probably hysterical paralysis."

In the end, Donna Love stood and walked. "When they told me Donna was going to walk," Stuart says, "I thought she was going to get physical therapy. I was totally surprised when she got up and walked across the room and pulled a flask out of a drawer and did a toast! I didn't even know she had a flask! I didn't know she drank in her bedroom!"

This led to Donna's last line on the soap's final episode. When Victoria sarcastically wondered if Donna were on the wagon, she turned to her and said, "I'm not."

After the demise of *Another World,* the characters of Jake and Victoria were transplanted to the CBS soap *As the World Turns.* Donna also popped up in Oakdale for a brief appearance in 1999.

Of Special Note: *Another World* was the first soap opera to generate a spin-off, *Somerset,* which premiered March 30, 1970. Perhaps because it had little in common with its parent show, *Somerset* went off the air in December 1976 after a mediocre ratings run. Its second spin-off, *Texas,* fared even worse, canceled after just more than two years.

Favorite Storyline: The May–December romance between Donna and Matt was particularly close to Stuart's heart. "I thought it was just a wonderful story. I thought it was such a good opportunity for humor and helped me be some kind of a role model for women in America who had the same dilemma in terms of aging and having fears surrounding that, and who happened to be involved with a young man, which made it all the more poignant.

"I think it appealed to women as a particular fantasy. I, for one, have never been drawn to young men. Never. That just hasn't been my thing. But so many women out there are drawn to the beauty of youth and maybe the innocence of youth. Maybe they're thinking, *If Donna can do it, so can I. Maybe there's someone out there who can save me from my terrible marriage.*

"I'm sorry they didn't choose to develop it further. I think it was safer to do the same old, same old of getting back with the ex-husband, but I think it would have been much more interesting to go on with Matt and Donna's relationship a little longer."

Real-Life Soap Opera: Although Stuart, who was born in Bluefield, West Virginia, might have found her niche playing Donna Love, she was already a popular soap actress long before she joined *Another World*. Anna made her daytime debut playing Toni Ferra Powers on *The Doctors,* a stint that lasted five years. From 1977 to 1979 she donned a stethoscope on *General Hospital* as Dr. Gina Dante before moving over to *Guiding Light* and assuming the character of Vanessa Chamberlain. According to Stuart, bouncing from soap to soap was fine with her. "My roles didn't end. I ended them."

When she was cast as Donna Love in 1983, she found the role that would become her signature and the character with whom she'll forever be most closely associated. Interestingly, Stuart's offcamera experiences on *Another World* are a mini soap opera in themselves. In 1986, Anna left the soap and was replaced by Philece Sampler. Then in 1989, Stuart was brought back. She admits she had some significant adjustments to make when she returned for the second go-round.

"When I left, my character was a glamorous, frivolous, troubled neurotic. She had all those little dimensions that made her so interesting. Maggie DePriest was the writer then and she wrote beautifully for Donna Love. Then, during my absence she was let go and Donna Swajeski was brought in. She was trying to write somebody else's idea of Donna Love, and she had to work with Philece Sampler, and Donna's dimensions got lost in the shuffle.

"Donna Swajeski," Stuart adds, "tried her very best to bury me and give me a hideous death. She just did not connect with Donna Love."

Stuart's real life, fortunately, is a lot less frenetic than Donna Love's.

"I find that the more I go along in life, the more I want to simplify," she says. "My idea of a party is going down to the pond and looking at the turtles and fish. It grounds me."

The pond of which she speaks is located at her country home, far from the maddening New York crowds. She shares the home with her longtime lover, actor Jesse Doran, who appeared on *Another World* as mobster Marius Sloan. They first met more than twenty years ago when she came upon his lost dog in a New York City park.

It seems Stuart has a knack for doing things in two shifts—she and Doran broke up for five years once, but ultimately got back together. And for Anna and Jesse, love is apparently better the second time around. They live together in a log cabin nestled next to the aforementioned pond and appear to live a charmed idyll.

"I didn't actually choose to live in a log cabin," Anna admits. "I actually had property we were going to build a house on, but a friend told me to look at this house. The driveway is quite long, so you really can't see anything from the road. Then as I drove down the driveway, I just fell in love with the property. It was so beautiful. But I still intended to build another house on it. Then by the time summer came around, I had also fallen in love with the log cabin so we never did build that house. We kept our log cabin instead."

The place offers Stuart the chance to relax into a more casual mode, a place to escape—and a place to be with family. The property has two houses, not to mention two barns. Anna and Jesse live in the main house, and her brother and his family live in the smaller house. Stuart enjoys puttering around and is proud of the work they've done on the house.

"Jesse's an actor, but when he's not working he does carpentry. He is very, very skilled and has really done a lot of work on the house. He built me a beautiful gazebo for my birthday from scratch. There aren't many people who can do that. But repair work like heating and plumbing isn't his forte so he leaves that to others. When my brother is available, he works with Jesse so it ends up being a family project, which is even nicer, because it's something we did ourselves together.

"Our home is a constant work in progress but there is a magic here. I would love to have this place forever and ever."

She would have loved to portray Donna for a longer time, too. But even though *Another World* is over, fans are still faithful to Stuart. "Yes, I'm still here," she says. "I'm hoping to take the tin cups that they are donating to each and every one of us and stick it out and hope that someone will put a piece of paper in it that says, 'I want you for a job!'

"I'm going to look for work; what would you do? I'm not wealthy enough to retire for the rest of my life, and even if I were, it's not my style. I've got way too far to go for that; I'd go crazy. Well, I probably wouldn't go crazy, but I'd hurt somebody," she smiles.

When asked about the youth-oriented bent of most soap operas today, Stuart swears it's not an issue for her. "I don't feel pressured at all. Maybe on bad days I go, *Oh, my God. Where is there a space for me?* But I really don't live in that place very often.

"But really, I was lucky on *Another World*. They gave me the story-line with a younger man and they didn't play it as if I was the aging woman lusting after youth. They did something genuine. And I kept saying, 'More! Let's do menopause! I want to do this while I have a young guy!' They did a menopause scare but let it go at that.

"I wanted to see Donna do all those things that everybody was afraid to deal with. Women don't want to acknowledge that they're getting older, that they're having hot flashes. I want to do all that. I'm game. I'm not one of those women who tries to hide her age."

She does, however, work at making sure she looks her best. "I don't drink, I don't smoke, I don't drink sodas, I eat a healthy diet, but that's a lifestyle for me; it's not like I'm on a diet. I work out, but it's a lifestyle, passed down to me by my mother from my grand-mother. It's just kind of a family thing. And I've got good genes, I guess. And I don't sleep well at night! Maybe that's the secret! Try staying up all night—see what happens! But you can't eat chocolate chip ice cream while you're doing it!"

Overall, Stuart seems content and settled into her life and accepts the process of getting older gracefully and with humor. "I have changed. I've mellowed. I really used to be into sex. Now, I'm into carbohydrates. This is a big change for me. The thing is, I'm a double Scorpio. I can be so up but I can also be so down. I've struggled many times in my life but I've always survived. I always come back and regenerate."

This may explain how she envisions celebrating her sixtieth birthday.

"When I'm 60 years old, I plan on draping myself across a piano, the way Shirley MacLaine did in *Postcards from the Edge,* and sing 'I'm Still Here' from *Follies.* Because I am still here."

Most Notable Real-Life Diva Moment: "I got hysterically blind once. I just couldn't see out of one eye for about six months, and then the eyesight in it came back."

Trivia: The first scene broadcast when *Another World* premiered in 1964 was of Irene Dailey, playing Liz Matthews, weeping over the death of her newly deceased husband.

Philece Sampler played the role of Donna during Stuart's leave of absence from the show.

Div-o-Meter: 4—It's hard to be too much of a diva in prison scrubs.

HUNTER TYLO

Hunter Tylo achieved real-life diva status by taking on mega-producer Aaron Spelling in a famous legal battle.

Crowning Role: Taylor Forrester on *The Bold and the Beautiful*

Reign: 1990–present

Other Notable Roles: Robin McCall on *All My Children* (1985–87) and Marina Toscano Johnson on *Days of Our Lives* (1989)

Character's Most Notable Pursuit: Playing ping-pong for Ridge Forrester's affections with Brooke Logan

Character's Occupation: Psychiatrist

Character's Full Name: Taylor Hamilton Hayes Forrester Rasheed Forrester

Husbands: Blake Hayes, Ridge Forrester, and Prince Omar Rasheed

Character's Diva-lution: Dr. Taylor Hayes moved to Los Angeles to start a new life apart from her ex-husband, Blake. Before her bags were unpacked, she ran into an old high school friend, Storm Logan, at a restaurant. When he found out she was divorced, Storm set out to romance Taylor, whom he had always had feelings for, even as a teenager.

Taylor accepted a job caring for Caroline Forrester, who was suffering from a fatal form of leukemia. Her first encounter with Caroline's husband, Ridge Forrester, was to tell him that his wife was dying. As she was nearing death, Caroline asked Taylor to be there for Ridge after she was gone.

After Caroline died, Taylor delivered a letter to Ridge from his deceased wife in which she asked him to go on with his life and find happiness. Trying to deal with his depression, Ridge frequently turned to Taylor for guidance and support, and their friendship began to deepen. Even though everyone seemed willing to confide in Taylor, she was very secretive about her past, particularly her relationship with Blake.

Storm's sister, Brooke Logan, had once been in love with Ridge and, in truth, was who Caroline had hoped Ridge would get together with after her death. It was Taylor, however, that Ridge began having romantic feelings for. Storm proposed to Taylor first, telling her to think about it for a week before giving him an answer.

In her heart, Taylor knew she was in love with Ridge, but they agreed not to see each other any longer out of concern for Storm. Storm eventually realized that Taylor wasn't in love with him, so he left L.A. and moved to San Francisco. Just as it seemed the path was clear for Ridge and Taylor to get together, her ex-husband, Blake, showed up and promptly began spying on her. Blake, who was prone to violent attacks if not on special medication, wanted Taylor back.

He set about to screw up her relationship with Ridge by making her think Ridge was really in love with Brooke.

When it was obvious that Taylor still only had eyes for Ridge, Blake left for Texas. As soap opera luck would have it, while there he stumbled across Caroline's secret twin sister, Faith, from whom she'd been separated at birth. He brought Faith—a dead ringer for the dead Caroline—back to L.A. hoping Ridge would fall in love with her.

Ridge's heart was elsewhere. By this time, he was back in love with Brooke and wanted to marry her. Trouble was, she was married to his father, Eric. Ridge realized he couldn't break up his father's family and broke off his relationship with Brooke. Now free, he went after Taylor once again. Though she was angry at first, she accepted his proposal. They were married the same day Brooke found out she was pregnant.

On her way to a conference, Taylor's plane crashed and she was presumed dead. In truth, she wasn't on the plane. During a layover, she'd been attacked by a mugger and taken to a local hospital. Because all of her belongings had been on the plane, she had no identification on her. And wouldn't you know, she awoke from the attack with amnesia.

Never one to be alone for long, Taylor was befriended by Prince Omar Rasheed, who gave her the name Princess Laila. When her memory came back, Taylor tried to leave, but the prince locked her up. Meanwhile, believing Taylor dead, Ridge married Brooke (who had meanwhile divorced Eric).

Cruelly, Omar arranged to have Ridge and Brooke spend their honeymoon in his country and fixed it so Taylor could observe them and see how much in love they were, in hopes of making her want to stay with him. Depressed, Taylor agreed to marry the prince, although they never consummated the marriage. When her picture as Princess Laila appeared in the paper, it was spotted by a friend of Taylor's from L.A., who confronted her but couldn't convince her to return to Los Angeles.

When she heard her father was near death, Taylor hopped a plane home and went to visit him in disguise. As fate would have it, Ridge was in the same hospital suffering from temporary blindness as the result of an accident at work. Because he couldn't see her, Taylor became a hospital volunteer and cared for him. Because he was still married to Brooke, Taylor intended to go back to the prince, but she changed her mind and finally revealed her true identity to Ridge. Not amused, the prince flew to L.A. to get his princess back. He didn't.

And Taylor didn't get Ridge, either. He served her with divorce papers so he could legally marry Brooke. Unable to see Ridge with Brooke, Taylor left for Paris. When she got back, she became enamored with Thorne, after he saved her from perishing in a house fire she accidentally set. Eventually, she and Ridge remarried.

Real-Life Soap Opera: Hunter Tylo was born Deborah Hunter Morehart on July 3, 1961, in Fort Worth, Texas, the third of four children. Part Cherokee Indian on her mother's side, Hunter says she grew up feeling ugly.

"I had big lips and eyes and was always teased. I hated makeup and didn't give a damn about boys."

Hoping to instill a little gentility in her daughter, Hunter says her mom "sent me to charm school. She just wanted me to grow up and be a little lady, because that's the Southern thing to do."

After she got out of school, Hunter worked as a model. She was briefly married and had a son, Christopher. The marriage ended in 1983. Hunter's modeling career led her into acting. One project she is less than proud of now was a low budget film in which she appeared nude. Years later, the film would come back to haunt her when stills from the movie were published in a magazine.

Tylo's first job in daytime was on *All My Children,* where she met her future husband, Michael Tylo. It was not exactly love at first sight.

"We had both kind of been let down by life . . . but we got to be friends. Then I thought, *Oh, he's not such a bad guy. In fact, I've got to take care of him!* That's how we started falling in love."

After marrying Michael in July 1987, Deborah Morehart legally changed her name to Hunter Tylo. The couple has three children together—Michael, Izabella, and Katya, who was born with a form of eye cancer called retinoblastoma. The experience was devastating for Hunter.

"You go through so many feelings. The first week Katya was diagnosed, I went from, 'This is too painful, I need to push this child away,' to the extreme, 'I better cling to this child, and I'm going to push my other children and my husband and everyone else away. And by God, I'm going to give this kid everything.' Then you feel guilty."

After chemotherapy and several surgeries, Katya is doing fine and doctors give her a hopeful prognosis. Meanwhile, Hunter and Michael have to concentrate on raising her just like any other child.

"Where we have been overprotective, we're correcting that," Tylo says. "She is a little spoiled. She fusses when she doesn't get her way, but for the most part, she's a very loving child.

"Katya goes to the hospital every three weeks to get blood drawn, and they check for everything. All the nurses know her. She runs and hugs them even though they're going to be sticking her with needles. They want to make sure the chemo hasn't triggered something else. There are all kinds of risks. Talk about having your faith stretched. You just have to trust that God has taken control."

Hunter says she has learned, "With life, you don't ever know what's going to happen. All you can do is be thankful for each of the good days and ask for help to get through the hard days."

Awards and Accolades: Tylo has twice been voted one of *People* magazine's 50 Most Beautiful People (1993 and 1998). She has also received a Best Actress Award and an MVP Award from *Soap Opera Update.*

Most Notable Real-Life Diva Moment: Suing producer Aaron Spelling for firing her from *Melrose Place* and starring in a very public trial.

In February 1996, Tylo was hired to appear on eight episodes of the steamy primetime soap, playing a woman trying to seduce Jack Wagner, Heather Locklear's husband on the show. Filming was scheduled to begin in July.

In March she discovered she was pregnant, and in April, the producers informed her via fax that she was dismissed from her contract on grounds of "material change in appearance." In other words, her pregnancy was "incompatible" with the vixenish role she had been hired to play.

Tylo sued, and the case went to trial in November. The jury of ten women and two men found that Spelling Entertainment Group and Spelling Television, Inc., had wrongfully terminated her and ordered the producers to pay $4 million for emotional distress and $894,601 for economic loss.

Tylo pronounced the verdict a victory "for every woman, for every child that's not born. I know a lot of actresses who are afraid to announce that they are thinking about having children because they are afraid of being written out or written down."

For his part, Aaron Spelling said, "I am really deeply hurt by all this. I don't mind being a target. I don't mind bad reviews for a show; critics have the right to say what they think. But I would bet you a dollar to your nickel, if you called any member of our casts, you'd find a love fest." Spelling argued that because Tylo hadn't yet appeared on the program, it made more sense to hire an actress they wouldn't have to film around. (Ironically, Lisa Rinna, the actress hired in Tylo's place, became pregnant during her tenure on the show but was not fired.) Spelling said that they had tried to reach a compromise with Tylo, offering her more money and a longer contract—on the next season. But she stuck to her guns and went to court.

Cause: Chosen Child, a charity begun by Hunter designed to provide prenatal health and fitness education to expectant mothers, as well as legal assistance to working mothers. Part of the funding will come from her settlement money from the *Melrose Place* case. Other monies will come from private donations and contributions from baby care product manufacturers.

Div-o-Meter: 8—because she fought the law—and won.

Famous Alumni

Although soap operas have often been thought the ugly stepsister of primetime, they have been the proven training ground for not only future primetime stars, but major motion picture actors as well. Soaps have moreover provided a home to many established actors who suddenly find roles in primetime and films hard to come by. Following is a list of some of the more noteworthy names of actors who are soap alumni:

Another World

GABRIELLE CARTERIS

FAITH FORD

THOMAS GIBSON

KELSEY GRAMMER

ANNE HECHE

MARY PAGE KELLER

AUDRA LINDLEY

RAY LIOTTA

VING RHAMES

ERIC ROBERTS

As the World Turns

JULIANNE MOORE

MEG RYAN

MARK RYDELL

MARISA TOMEI

MING-NA WEN

The Bold and the Beautiful

JEFF CONAWAY

JAMES DOOHAN

TIPPI HEDREN

Dark Shadows

KATE JACKSON

Days of Our Lives

MIKE FARRELL

MARY FRANN

CHARLES SHAUGHNESSY

JOAN VAN ARK

The Doctors

ARMAND ASSANTE

ALEC BALDWIN

JULIA DUFFY

JONATHAN FRAKES

KATHLEEN TURNER

General Hospital

RICHARD DEAN ANDERSON

DEMI MOORE

JAMES SIKKING

ROY THINNES

Guiding Light

KEVIN BACON

RUBY DEE

MELINA KANAKAREDES

JOHN WESLEY SHIPP

SHERRY STRINGFIELD

BILLY DEE WILLIAMS

IAN ZIERING

Love Is a Many Splendored Thing

DAVID BIRNEY

DONNA MILLS

Love of Life

BONNIE BEDELIA

PAUL MICHAEL GLASER

TONY LOBIANCO

CHRISTOPHER REEVE

ROY SCHEIDER

FRANCES STERNHAGEN

JESSICA WALTER

Loving

CELESTE HOLM

PATRICIA KALEMBER

LUKE PERRY

TERI POLO

One Life to Live

TOM BERENGER

ROMA DOWNEY

TOMMY LEE JONES

JUDITH LIGHT

Ryan's Hope

CATHERINE HICKS

EARL HINDMAN

KATE MULGREW

CHRISTIAN SLATER

Somerset

TED DANSON

AUDREY LANDERS

JAMESON PARKER

The Young and the Restless

VIVICA A. FOX

DAVID HASSELHOFF

WINGS HAUSER

BRIAN KERWIN

TOM SELLECK

FOREST WHITAKER

MARCY WALKER

Though Santa Barbara *is long gone, Eden Castillo is still one of the most beloved characters in soap history.*

Crowning Role: Eden Capwell on *Santa Barbara*

Reign: 1984–92

Other Notable Roles: Liza Colby on *All My Children* (1981–84, 1995–present) and Tangie Hill on *Guiding Light* (1993–95)

Character's Most Notable Pursuit: Sanity

Character's Full Name: Eden Capwell Cranston Castillo

Husbands: Kirk Cranston and Cruz Castillo

Character's Diva-lution: Eden Capwell arrived in Santa Barbara in October 1984, by accidentally parachuting onto the Lockridge estate, the home of her family's arch enemies. Eden had spent the previous five years getting over the death of her brother, Channing

Capwell (who, it was eventually revealed, had been accidentally killed by his mother, Sophia).

At a birthday party thrown in honor of her father, C. C., Eden met Cruz Castillo. It was not love at first sight. It turned out that Eden and Cruz had met each other in Paris and enjoyed a brief romance. He was definitely from the wrong side of the tracks for her wealthy family, so once back home, they maintained a distance.

They did, however, become partners in an effort to find a sunken ship. While on a dive, Eden almost drowned, and afterward she and Cruz kissed for the first time. It was the start of a classic star-crossed lovers saga—and the start of mind-boggling bad luck for Eden.

In 1986, the "Carnation Killer" kidnapped Eden, who was rescued by Cruz. It was obvious they still had feelings for each other. Cruz proposed to Eden, but she was afraid of committing to him—until he was almost killed. Coming so close to losing Cruz made her realize just how much she loved him. So, she lured him into the woods, where she proposed to him and he accepted.

Their plans went up in flames, as it were, when a fire forced them to postpone their wedding. Then just as they were preparing for the next time, Cruz arrested Eden's mother for the murder of Channing. C. C. then intervened and got them back together.

C. C. suffered a stroke, and Gina, who wanted Eden to pull the plug on her father, drugged Eden at her engagement party. Later, Eden believed that she did indeed try to kill her dad. C. C. recovered, but Eden broke up with Cruz, unable to face him because of what she thought she did. Instead, she married Kirk Cranston, an associate from Capwell Industries who was playing mind games with Eden.

Jealous of Eden's continued feelings for Cruz, Kirk blew up a cabin with Cruz and Eden inside. Cruz backed off once he found out that Eden was pregnant with Kirk's baby. Instead, he married Santana.

Kirk figured out that Gina had pulled the plug on C. C., and he blackmailed Gina into trying to kill Eden. Eden fought back, and in the struggle, Gina fell into the ocean and was presumed drowned. The shock of these events caused Eden to have a car accident and she subsequently lost the baby. Eventually, Kirk again tried to kill Eden, but Cruz saved her and Kirk was arrested.

Cruz and Eden were reunited, but they broke up again after she found out that he slept with his old girlfriend, Tori—even though it happened while Cruz and Tori were shipwrecked, and in his delirium he thought he was making love to Eden. Tori became pregnant and gave birth to a son, Chip.

After a few more break-ups and reconciliations, Cruz and Eden were finally married on April 1, 1988. Not long afterward, Chip needed a bone marrow transplant and Tori was forced to tell Cruz that he was Chip's father. Tori eventually entered a drug rehab clinic and gave custody of Chip to Cruz and Eden.

More heartbreak was ahead. Eden was raped and soon discovered she was pregnant. To the surprise of everyone, the baby turned out to be Cruz's, not the rapist's. After Eden gave birth to her daughter, Adriana, the rapist, who turned out to be Eden's doctor, kidnapped the child. Cruz and Eden eventually found their baby in Paris.

Their happiness, however, was short-lived. Eden became infatuated with an old lover, Robert Barr, causing her and Cruz to temporarily separate. In 1990, Cruz's investigation of a drug ring led to an attempt on Eden's life. Eden ended up in a coma. The ringleader turned out to be none other than bad-man-around-town Kirk Cranston.

Later that year, Eden shot Robert's evil twin, Quinn, in self-defense. When her sister Kelly was arrested for the murder, Eden had no choice but to come forward. On her way to the police, though, she was in yet another car accident and wound up in yet another coma. After a spiritual experience, in which Cruz brought her back from the brink of death, the real murderer, Quinn's ex-girlfriend, was revealed.

Eden recovered her physical health, but her emotional state was degenerating. When a man from her past, a jewel thief named Andre, came to town, Eden developed multiple personalities—Lisa, also a jewel thief—her brother Channing, and Suzanne Collier.

Lisa, the dominant personality, faked Eden's death and returned in disguise as Suzanne. When Eden's mother, Sophia, finally figured out Suzanne was Eden, Eden became Channing and shot Sophia as revenge for his death twelve years before. After failing in her attempt to kill Sophia, "Suzanne" left town. After Cruz received divorce papers supposedly sent from Eden, he resigned himself to starting over and he began a relationship with Kelly.

Of Special Note: Santa Barbara fans rose up in protest over the way producers chose to end the Cruz/Eden storyline once Walker announced she was leaving the show.

Real-Life Soap Opera: Marcy Walker comes from Smoky Mountain country, although she didn't get to spend much time there. Her father's job as a field service engineer required the family to constantly be on the move. Not only did Marcy live all over the United States growing up, she also spent time in Iran and Switzerland.

After graduating from high school in Illinois, she briefly attended college at Southern Illinois University. She moved to New York, and at age eighteen she was cast as scheming teen Liza Colby on *All My Children*. Three years later, Walker joined a new soap, *Santa Barbara,* as the really long-suffering Eden Capwell. The romance between Eden and Cruz, played by A Martinez, became one of the most famous and beloved in soap history.

After spreading her wings and starring in a few primetime TV movies, including *The Return of Desperado, Bar Girls,* and *Midnight Child,* Walker left *Santa Barbara,* which went off the air a year later.

By 1993, Walker was ready to return to daytime. She joined *Guiding Light* as Tangie Hill, a love interest for Josh Lewis, who was still grieving his presumed dead wife, Reva. The experience left her underwhelmed because of her character's weak storylines. In looking back, she feels she was hired mostly as a trophy.

"Certain performers," she explains, "can bring a show validity or interest in the press, but it doesn't serve the actor. They end up taking the job under the guise of being used as part of the repertoire and then they're not used. That show didn't need me."

So, in 1995 when *All My Children* approached her to reprise her role as Liza, Walker didn't hesitate. "I knew I was being asked to join *AMC* because of what I do, and not because of who I am."

Going "back home" has recharged Marcy. "It was like going into a time machine. Everyone's there—there are so many familiar faces. And working with Michael Knight [Tad] is a blast. We're old friends. We originally screen-tested together back in 1982."

Favorite soap characters, however, are not easily forgotten. In September 1996, A Martinez and Marcy were reunited at the *Soap Opera Digest* Awards as presenters and the audience went wild.

Awards and Accolades: Twice nominated for Daytime Emmy Awards in the Best Supporting Actress category for *All My Children,* Walker took home an Emmy statuette (and another nomination) for Best Actress for *Santa Barbara.* Walker and A Martinez were named Outstanding Supercouple by *Soap Opera Digest* in 1990, and Walker won the magazine's Outstanding Supporting Actress Award for *All My Children* in 1997.

Most Notable Real-Life Diva Moment: Walker's personal marital history reads almost like a soap character's. By the time she was just thirty years old, she had been married and divorced three times and had a child out of wedlock.

Her first (brief) marriage was to actor Stephen Ferris, followed by *Days of Our Lives* star Billy Warlock in 1987. After that marriage dissolved, Walker became involved with a cameraman named Stephan Collins. They had a child together in 1989, married a year later, and divorced soon after. Next, she married audio technician Robert Primrose, whom she met on the set of *Guiding Light.* That marriage also ended in divorce.

"I think everybody loves to be in love. But now I've come to the point where I say if I don't know what marriage is, I shouldn't be married," she has commented. That said, in October 1999, Marcy announced her engagement to Doug Smith.

Trivia: In a flashback sequence on *Santa Barbara,* Leonardo DiCaprio played Mason Capwell as a young boy in one of his first television guest appearances.

Div-o-Meter: 8—just on the sheer strength of the enduring legacy of Eden.

JESS WALTON

Jill Foster Abbott (Jess Walton) is at her best when sparring with Kay Chancellor—in daytime's longest-running feud.

Crowning Role: Jill Foster Abbott on *The Young and the Restless*

Reign: 1987–present

Other Notable Roles: Shelley Granger, aka Kelly Harper, on *Capitol* (1984–87)

What Jess Says About Jill: "Jill has an itch and it can never be satisfied by any one man. She gets bored very easily and has to keep moving. She's a great fault-finder in people."

Character's Most Notable Pursuit: Bitch-fighting with Katherine and making sure her marriages are legal

Character's Full Name: Jill Foster Brooks Abbott Abbott

Husbands: Phillip Chancellor II (marriage later deemed illegal), Brock Reynolds (also deemed illegal), Derek Thurston (annulled), Stuart Brooks (divorced), Rex Sterling (also deemed illegal), and John Abbott (married and divorced twice)

Character's Diva-lution: In her early days, Jill Foster was a woman of modest means, working as a manicurist at the local beauty salon. Her life would change when she befriended Genoa City's grande dame, Katherine "Kay" Chancellor, who had plenty of money but nary a friend.

Unlikely allies, Kay and Jill became the town odd couple, and eventually, Kay hired Jill to be her live-in assistant. It wasn't long before Kay's husband, Phillip, found himself attracted to the young woman living under their roof.

Life at the Chancellor manse became difficult. Whenever Kay was drunk or in a foul mood, she would blame Jill for anything and everything that went wrong. The truth was, Kay was worried that Phillip simply didn't love her anymore. And she was right. He loved Jill. And Jill, in return, found herself falling in love with him, and they began an affair.

Although it had been his intention to remain married, Phillip realized he didn't want to live a shadowed life with Jill so he left Genoa City to file for divorce. When he returned after the divorce was final, Katherine picked him up from the airport and on the way, got into a car crash. Although he was gravely injured, Phillip and Jill were married in his hospital room. Moments later, Phillip died. Jill and Kay bitterly blamed the other for Phillip's death and therein began the feud that would last decades. Because Phillip's divorce from Kay was fraudulently obtained, his marriage to Jill was invalid, and thus she lost out on inheriting the Chancellor estate.

Jill has also had other headaches besides Kay, such as her illegal marriage to Brock Reynolds (Kay's son from her marriage to Gary Reynolds), an invalid marriage to Rex Sterling (who was still legally wed to Kay at the time), or the marriage with Derek Thurston that was annulled, or her marriage and subsequent divorce from Stuart Brooks. Or the time businessman Victor Newman was shot and she was arrested for it, her assumed motive being that Victor was siding with her ex-husband John Abbott in a bitter custody battle over their son, Billy. Jill was cleared, however, when the ballistics test proved she hadn't fired a gun.

The core of Jill's existence is still her running feud with Kay, which tends to hide the fact that in a strange way, Kay and Jill really couldn't live without each other.

Of Special Note: Prior to Walton's reign, the character of Jill was played by Brenda Dickson (1973–80, 1983–87), Bond Gideon (1980), and Deborah Adair (1980–83).

Real-Life Soap Opera: Jess Walton was born a Great Lakes Midwesterner in Grand Rapids, Michigan, but was raised a Canuck in Toronto, Ontario, Canada. Her interest in acting began when Jess was nine after she participated in a summer camp play.

After finishing her scholastic education, Jess studied acting at the Toronto Workshop Productions' Repertory Theater for three years. Through her performances in shows such as *Uncle Vanya* and *The Right Honorable Gentleman,* Jess was featured on the cover of *Canadian TV Guide.*

Walton moved to Los Angeles after being signed by the William Morris talent agency and became a contract player for Universal Studios. While there, she guest-starred in a variety of series, including

Cannon, Kojak, The Six Million Dollar Man, The Rockford Files, Ironside, Starsky and Hutch, Barnaby Jones, Gunsmoke, and *Marcus Welby, M.D.,* and she appeared in the features *The Fortunate Painter, The Storm,* and *The Peace Killers.*

Just as her career was blossoming, though, Jess took a three-year hiatus from acting after her son, Cole, was born.

"I am glad I did that," she says now, "because I never could have gotten those years back."

Nor did the sabbatical damage her career. As soon as she started going back on auditions, she landed the role of former prostitute Shelley Granger on *Capitol.* Then in 1987, she won the role that would change her professional life—the "new" Jill Foster Abbott, replacing Brenda Dickson in the role.

Walton is married to John W. James, founder of the internationally known Grief Recovery Institute and author of the best-selling book *The Grief Recovery Handbook.*

Although to some her husband's work may seem more "important" than soap stardom, Walton's son, Cole, helped her put her work as an actress in perspective. "Once I was talking about how John changes people's lives," recalls Walton, "and Cole said, 'Don't ever put down what you do, Mom. You give a lot of people something.'"

Awards and Accolades: The character of Jill won Jess two Emmy Awards, one as Outstanding Supporting Actress (1991) and one as Outstanding Actress (1997). She also won a *Soap Opera Digest* Award as Outstanding Actress (1993).

Div-o-Meter: 9—Although she can hold her own with the likes of Jeanne Cooper's Kay Chancellor, Jess needs just a little more edge.

RUTH WARRICK

*The always fabulous Ruth Warrick plays
the occasionally fatuous Phoebe Wallingford.*

Crowning Role: Phoebe Wallingford on *All My Children*

Reign: 1970–present

Other Notable Roles: Janet Johnson on *Guiding Light* (1953–54),
Edith Hughes on *As the World Turns* (1956–60)

What Ruth Says About Phoebe: "People like the strength of
Phoebe, although to begin with I thought of her as a silly person
whose most strenuous activity was stirring the martinis gently so as
not to bruise the gin. I had been involved with the civil rights and
peace movements—a really involved activist—and she was the
opposite, so I made her a really ridiculous bubblehead.

"After a few months, the director said to me, 'Your role is to
make people afraid of you. When you walk into a room, they
should soil their pants.' That's when Phoebe got very heavy. She

was so outrageous you wanted to kill her, but she became a woman with spirit and spunk and spine."

Character's Full Name: Phoebe English Tyler Wallingford Matthews Wallingford

Husbands: Charles Tyler, Langley Wallingford, and Wade Matthews

Character's Diva-lution: Known as the biggest gossip and meddler in Pine Valley, Phoebe's own life is the stuff of tabloid dreams.

At the show's debut in 1970, Phoebe was introduced as the snobby, blue blood wife of Dr. Charles Tyler, the chief of staff of Pine Valley Hospital. Her two main pastimes were pointing out the foibles of others and endlessly butting in to the private lives of her children, Lincoln (Linc) and Anne, and teenage grandson, Chuck. Phoebe would finally meet her match in Chuck's social-climbing girlfriend, Erica Kane, the daughter of Charles's secretary, Mona Kane.

Phoebe was so busy paying attention to everyone else's life that she didn't notice that her husband was drifting away from her and falling in love with Mona. When Charles asked for a divorce in 1976, Phoebe refused. Phoebe's meddling, however, would be her downfall. That same year, in a desperate attempt to prevent Linc from remarrying lounge singer Kitty Shea, Phoebe hired an impostor to pose as the girl's long-lost mother, Lucy Carpenter. When Mona, who knew Lucy, met the impostor, Myrtle, she discovered the scam and blackmailed Phoebe into granting Charles a divorce.

Three years later, Phoebe was the victim of a scam herself when she married a carnival worker posing as respected professor Langley Wallingford. Then, in 1986, Phoebe married the much younger Wade Matthews, another con artist who tried to kill Phoebe for her money. Eventually, she reconciled with Langley, whom she loved despite his humble beginnings.

These days, Phoebe contents herself with occasionally meddling in the affairs of others—particularly her niece Brooke—and with being a founding member of the Daughters of Fine Lineage, an exclusive ladies' organization.

Real-Life Soap Opera: Ruth Warrick was born in St. Joseph, Missouri, on June 29, 1915. As a teenager, she moved to Kansas City. After graduating the University of Kansas City, she traveled to New York, where in 1939 she became part of television history.

"I did the first in-house test of TV in the RCA Building, a little spiel about the possibilities of TV that was transmitted from one end of the building to the other," she recalls. "I remember the lights were gosh-awful. I got burns on my face, that's how strong they were, and the tears were streaming down, though they couldn't be seen because the picture was a little fuzzy."

The turning point in her life and career came when she met Orson Welles, who was then running the Mercury Theater. When Welles headed west for Hollywood, the auburn-haired, blue-eyed Warrick followed. In 1941, she appeared in three films, *Obliging Young Lady, The Corsican Brothers,* and the now classic *Citizen Kane,* in which she played Welles's distant wife.

Although their onscreen relationship was frosty, Warrick has since admitted that their personal ties were more heated. "I loved him," she admits. "It wasn't just a crush. I adored him, although I never let myself do anything about it.

"Orson sent for me a couple of times after the picture ended, and I did go one time, but I realized what the situation was and what he wanted from me and what would undoubtedly have happened. I was a married woman and I had a baby. I would have adored it, but I just couldn't do it because I'm a lady."

Over the next thirteen years, Warrick worked steadily in films such as *Let's Dance, Journey into Fear, Forever and a Day, Song of the South,*

Three Husbands, and *Beauty on Parade.* Eventually tiring of the roles being offered, Warrick returned to New York in 1954, hoping to revive her theater career. She appeared with Jackie Gleason in *Take Me Along* and toured in *Irene.* It was in the upstart medium of television that Warrick would find her greatest professional success, beginning with an offer to join the daytime serial *Guiding Light.*

"People said, 'My God, Ruth, you've ruined your career. How can Mrs. Citizen Kane be on a soap, for God's sake?'" Warrick recalls. "I said, 'Darn it, I need the job. I have to put my children through college.'"

Guiding Light, which had started as a radio serial in 1937, debuted on television in 1952 and was the only radio show to successfully make the transition to the small screen. Its creator, Irna Phillips, would go on to create another popular soap, *As the World Turns,* which premiered on April 2, 1956. Phillips cast Warrick in his new soap as Edith Hughes, the sister of the main character, Chris Hughes. In a controversial (for the times) storyline, Edith was having an affair with her brother's married law firm partner.

Warrick left the soap after five years. After appearing in the film *Father of the Bride,* she returned to television again when she was cast in what would prove to be the first successful primetime soap opera, *Peyton Place.* The now legendary cast of the show included Mia Farrow, Ryan O'Neal, Dorothy Malone, Leigh Taylor-Young, Dan Duryea, Ruby Dee, Diana Hyland, Lee Grant, Gena Rowlands, and Mariette Hartley. *Peyton Place* ran for five seasons until June 1969. It wrapped just in time for Warrick to be offered the role that would become her signature character, Phoebe Tyler on *All My Children,* which premiered January 5, 1970.

When not working on *All My Children,* Warrick continued to appear in television guest spots and also devoted her time to championing many favorite causes, including arts-in-education programs for children in underprivileged areas. Warrick was a co-founder of Operation Bootstrap in Watts, where she taught communication skills. She has been a Dropout Prevention consultant for the Department of Labor under President John F. Kennedy and for the Job Training Corps under President Johnson. She also taught at Manhattan's Julia Richman High School as part of President Carter's City in Schools program.

A firm believer that you're never to old to keep learning, in 1991, Warrick received her certification as a licensed metaphysical teacher from Unity School of Practical Christianity in Lees Summit, Missouri.

Awards and Accolades: In 1983, Ruth received the first national Arts in Education Award from the Board of Directors of Business and Industry for Arts in Education, Inc. The award was renamed the Ruth Warrick Award for Arts in Education and is now given annually.

In 1995, she was given the first St. Joseph Proud Award for her work with youth.

Most Notable Real-Life Diva Moment: In 1993, Warrick became a central figure in a murder investigation that had all of Manhattan watching. An Indian prince and his Brazilian-born wife were found dead in their lavish Park Avenue apartment, setting into motion a mystery that initially left detectives baffled.

Prince Chitresh Rao Khedker, called Teddy, and his wife, Nenescha, had last been seen alive on a Friday afternoon. Their bodies were found by a maid the following Monday morning. Khedker's body was found on the living room floor, with an unexplained bloody puncture wound to his neck. His wife, who was found in the bedroom, had no visible wounds.

In the days following the discovery, police sources expressed confidence that it was a murder-suicide, but as the investigation wore on, it became clear that it was a double murder.

The autopsy showed that the prince and his wife had been stran-
gled, and the wound in the prince's neck was probably caused by a
belt during the attack. Although the apartment bore no sign of
forced entry, the couple's immaculate apartment, decorated with
Persian rugs on the walls, had been obviously rifled.

Investigators combing through the apartment found a steamy,
passionate love letter written to Khedker by Ruth Warrick, then
seventy-seven. The prince was fifty-seven.

Warrick and Khedker had been known friends for many years,
with Khedker frequently boasting about various television projects
he and Warrick allegedly had in the works.

After hearing about the deaths, Warrick released a statement,
which read in part, "They were elegant, aristocratic, generous, and
very private. . . . It seems so unfair that such gracious people
should have such a ghoulish demise. It is so sad that in such a troubled world, there cannot be more love than violence. I shall miss
them both very much."

The Manhattan police went out of their way to stress that
Warrick was not considered a suspect. They simply hoped that,
because of her close relationship to the prince, she might help them
formulate some leads.

Inevitably, news of the love letter that first led police to Warrick
leaked out, causing people to look at Warrick in a new light. Gossip
maven Liz Smith noted: "We don't wish to make light of a terrible situation but I must say that the steamy love note written by actress Ruth
Warrick to the late prince was certainly inspiring! Miss Warrick, who
was in *Citizen Kane* with Orson Welles, and who has reigned as a daytime soap diva on ABC's *All My Children* for many years, is 77 years
old. And brother, is she ever the living proof that after the Middle
Ages comes the Renaissance. More power to Ruth and to all women
who don't give up after the first or second bloom of youth fades."

When detectives finally solved the mystery, it was a plot that even a soap writer couldn't have dreamed up. Charged with the murders were George Cobo and Tony Lee Simpson, former lovers who later implicated each other as the killer, with the motive being robbery. Khedker had told the doorman to let the pair up, apparently believing one of them was an antiques dealer.

At the trial, Cobo's attorney argued that his client was a battered spouse who stood by and watched as his male lover murdered the prince and his wife out of fear of losing the man he loved. The attorney also said that Cobo finally turned Simpson in after he feared Simpson would leave him for a woman.

Although the trial was very high profile in New York, Warrick's relationship with the prince was never brought up in the proceedings. By then, her legend as a passionate woman of a certain age was fully cemented.

Div-o-Meter: 7—Her regal bearing is tempered by her social consciousness.

VICTORIA WYNDHAM

*Victoria Wyndham took over the role of
Rachel Cory from fellow diva Robin Strasser.*

Crowning Role: Rachel Cory on *Another World*

Reign: 1972–99

Other Notable Roles: Charlotte Waring Bauer on *Guiding Light* (1967–70)

What Victoria Says About Rachel: "She might have been naughty, but she was never psychotic. And on the whole I think Rachel has been a pretty interesting character and has enough varied storylines to keep me pretty interested or I wouldn't have stayed."

Character's Most Notable Pursuit: Protecting her backside from her stepdaughter, Iris

Character's Occupations: Restaurateur, sculptor, and publishing executive

Character's Full Name: Rachel Davis Matthews Clark Frame
Cory Cory Cory Hutchins

Husbands: Russell Matthews, Ted Clark, Steve Frame, Mackenzie
Cory, and Carl Hutchins

Character's Diva-lution: When Rachel first came to Bay City in
1967, she was your no-doubt-about-it bad girl—a would-be model
out to manipulate everything and everyone for her own gain. She
married Russ Matthews for the money she thought he had, but when
he didn't have it, she dumped him for Ted Clark. Rachel and Ted
opened a restaurant but neither the eatery nor the marriage lasted
long.

Not one to be without a man for very long, Rachel next became
obsessed with Steve Frame and participated in a long-lasting compe-
tition with Alice Matthews for his affections. When Rachel became
pregnant with Steve's baby, it looked as if she had won for good, but
Steve could never completely commit to Rachel. Even after they
divorced and Rachel had married Mac Cory—twice—she and Steve
wavered.

Although Rachel truly loved Mac, their relationship turned tem-
pestuous, in large part thanks to Mac's daughter, Iris, who hated
Rachel and did everything in her power to break Rachel and Mac up.
In one of Iris's more despicable moments, she was partly responsible
for Rachel miscarrying Mac's child by doing nothing to help even
though she knew Rachel needed medical assistance.

After the miscarriage, things were never the same between Mac
and Rachel. For a while, she tried to distract herself by becoming a
sculptor. The very night that Rachel had her first showing, however,
Mac went off for a one-night stand. They weathered that marital

storm, but when Rachel caught Mac in bed with another woman, the marriage teetered on the brink of collapse.

After Rachel gave birth to Mac's daughter, Amanda, Iris was more hell-bent than ever on destroying her stepmother. She never missed a chance to give Rachel bad advice, which ultimately led to Mac and Rachel divorcing. Iris's machinations could not keep them apart, however, and they remarried. Only then did Rachel realize she was pregnant from an affair she'd had with Mitch.

Rachel confronted Mitch—and accidentally shot him. When he fell over from the force of the injury, he caused a fire that burned down the building. Rachel was charged with murder. She went to prison, but was released when it was revealed that Mitch was still alive. And when he returned to Bay City, Rachel left Mac to be with him.

That ended when—surprise!—Steve Frame came back to town. Rachel and Steve remarried, but after Steve was killed in a car accident Rachel turned her attention back to Mac, and once again they married.

The man who would finally replace Mac in Rachel's heart was Carl Hutchins, although his first impression wasn't that stellar. He initiated their relationship by kidnapping Rachel in order to get back at his sworn enemy, Mac Cory. After Mac died, Rachel and Carl realized they were in love. They married, and in 1997, they had twins, Elizabeth and Cory.

Rachel endured yet another kidnapping, this time by Carl's mortal enemy, Alexander Nikos, but she was returned unharmed. Carl "died" several apparent deaths, but each time turned up alive and well, sometimes after long absences. In *Another World*'s last weeks on the air, Carl returned after being believed dead for more than a year. Rachel was stunned (you'd think she'd be used to it by now), but thrilled, and the couple renewed their wedding vows.

Of Special Note: During the time Rachel was pursuing sculpting, she created a nude statue of Carl. As it happens, Wyndham actually does sculpt and has presented shows in a number of cities, including New York and Washington, D.C. So, when the story called for Rachel to sculpt Carl, Victoria made the prop herself—although she says she merely used her imagination to complete it instead of having her costar Charles Keating pose in the nude.

Real-Life Soap Opera: Victoria Wyndham made her professional debut as an understudy in the Broadway production of *Fiddler on the Roof.* She followed that with a number of other stage credits before landing her first daytime role on *Guiding Light,* originating the character Charlotte Waring Bauer.

Ironically, she originally turned down the chance to play Rachel Cory when first asked, primarily because she didn't like the way the character had been portrayed as a villain during Robin Strasser's reign.

"I'd already quit a comparable role on *Guiding Light,*" explains Wyndham. "I wanted to play a real person, not another three-note character."

The soap's producers were willing to give Rachel a change of heart so Wyndham capitulated and signed on. Besides enjoying the challenge of transforming Rachel, working in daytime was extremely compatible with Wyndham's offcamera life.

"You have to remember, I was also a mother with two children," Victoria points out. "It's a great gig for a working actress who wants to bring up her children and be home every night.

"You know, when you go off to do movies, you might be away from your family from six weeks to a year. With nighttime you may be away for six weeks, and that was more time away from my family then I ever wanted to spend. *Another World* provided me with a very nice living where I could stay home and be home with my children every night and do homework and be a regular Mom. That seemed like a better alternative then gadding about and pursuing a career. The kids seemed more important than the career."

Plus, the job had the added advantage of being located in New York. "I didn't want to bring my children up in California," she says candidly. "We're an East Coast family," she says unapologetically.

So, for twenty-seven years, Wyndham was a fixture in daytime and her primary notoriety will always be *Another World*. Being one of the show's more enduring cast members, Wyndham was quite candid in recent years about the show losing its direction. She seemed to sense that the new generation of writers and producers were digging its grave.

"They don't know the history of the show," she complained. "They hire writers who don't know the history of the show, and then weird things happen. Their point of view is they don't think that there is any reason to really care about the history of a soap. That's the common wisdom.

"Unfortunately, there seems to be a major mindset among the television executives that says, *We want new viewers. We don't care about the old viewers.* Generations of people watch these shows and to say, *Well, we don't care about the old fans* strikes me as being extraordinarily short sighted. Why wouldn't you care about the fans? They are the ones that have kept your show on the air all of these years."

That single-minded goal to appeal to young viewers is exactly why NBC spared the even-lower-rated *Sunset Beach* and canceled *Another World* to make way for the new youth-oriented soap *Passions*.

Whether Wyndham will surface on another soap remains to be seen, although she certainly doesn't lack for things to keep her busy. Wyndham has myriad other interests, including the aforementioned sculpting. Some of her pieces are included in the permanent collection of the Smithsonian Institute.

Wyndham has shown and owned horses since childhood and was even invited a few years ago to ride in the prestigious United States Equestrian Team Final Selection Trials for the Olympics and in the National Horse Show at Madison Square Garden.

Victoria is also very gifted musically and wrote the libretto for the full-length ballet *Winter Dreams.* And just to show she's just as comfortable behind the camera as she is in front of it, Wyndham has directed several rock music videos.

"I'm one of those driven people," Wyndham says with Diva understatement. "I love to be busy—and sleep deprived."

Awards and Accolades: Victoria has received three Emmy nominations for Outstanding Actress and two Best Actress *Soap Opera Digest* Awards.

Most Notable Real-Life Diva Moment: Initially turning down the role of Rachel because she didn't want to play a villain—the way Robin Strasser had been playing the role.

Trivia: This role was originated by another diva, **Robin Strasser** (see pages 157–165), who played Rachel in two stints, from 1967 to 1971 and again in 1972. Prior to Wyndham's arrival, Margie Impert took over the role temporarily.

In 1995, Wyndham took on the second role of Rachel look-alike Justine Duvalier, who tried to steal Rachel's life.

Div-o-Meter: 8—Anyone who can get away with dissing another Diva's portrayal of the same role—as Wyndham indirectly did of Strasser's depiction of Rachel—has got blue blood running through her veins. But Victoria isn't quite in-your-face enough to join the likes of Lucci and McKinsey atop the Diva heap.

KIM ZIMMER

Kim Zimmer's Reva may have married all the Lewis men, but her heart belongs only to Josh.

Crowning Role: Reva Shayne on *Guiding Light*

Reign: 1983–90, 1995–present

Other Notable Roles: Nola Aldrich on *The Doctors* (1979–82); Echo DiSavoy on *One Life to Live* (1983); and Jodie Walker on *Santa Barbara* (1992–93)

What Kim Says About Reva: "I've still never found a role that challenged me like Reva."

Character's Most Notable Pursuit: Dumping one Lewis man for another in his immediate family

Character's Occupations: Nurse's aide, photographer, and employee of Lewis Oil

Character's Full Name: Reva Shayne Lewis Lewis Spaulding Lewis Cooper Lewis

Husbands: Harlan Billy Lewis II, Harlan Billy Lewis I, Alan Spaulding (annulled), Joshua Lewis, and Frank Achilles "Buzz" Cooper

Character's Diva-lution: Reva Shayne knows how to get the most out of a marriage. When her college sweetheart, Joshua Lewis, had the audacity to leave her to go to college, Reva got back at him by marrying his brother Billy, whom she later divorced. She came to Springfield in 1983 as part of Alan Spaulding's plan to break up Billy and Vanessa. After announcing—falsely—that their divorce was never finalized, Reva demanded $5 million to divorce Billy. While in Springfield, her romance with Josh was rekindled, but once her deceit was revealed, she lost both the $5 million and Josh, who dumped her out of disgust.

If Josh didn't want her, she'd just find a Lewis who did. This time, she set her sights on the much older H. B. Lewis, Josh and Billy's father. They married and she soon got pregnant. She then lost H. B.'s child after Vanessa, under the influence of tranquilizers, ran her over with a car.

Reva and H. B. split up when she fell in love with Kyle Sampson (who turned out to be Billy Lewis's half brother). Kyle, however, would break her heart by dumping her for his former girlfriend, Maeve Stoddard. When Kyle married Maeve, Reva tried to kill herself by jumping off a bridge.

After recovering from her unsuccessful suicide attempt, Reva was briefly involved with Alan Spaulding. When that didn't work out, she was reunited with Josh and they were finally married. Then, the birth of their second child, Shayne, resulted in severe post-partum depression. In 1990, she drove her car off a bridge in Florida and was presumed dead.

Five years later, Alan found Reva living incognito as Rebecca Blume in an Amish community. Once her true identity was revealed, Reva came back to Springfield to pick up the pieces of her life. While she was gone, Joshua had married Annie Dutton—so Reva found a new romance of her own with Frank "Buzz" Cooper.

Nothing, however, could dampen the love Josh and Reva had for each other. Their passion was obvious to everyone, especially Annie. Desperate to hold onto Josh, Annie got pregnant through artificial insemination. When she miscarried, Annie flung herself down a flight of stairs and accused Reva of having done it. The truth came out at Reva's trial, and she was exonerated. Annie, however, was just getting started.

Determined to ruin Reva, Annie teamed up with Alan and Reva's long lost sister, Cassie, to destroy the Lewises. In the end, Annie took the more direct route of kidnapping Reva, locking her in a plane and sending her off to die in a plane crash.

Once again presuming her to be dead, a grief-stricken Josh had Reva cloned. Reva, though, was very much alive. She had survived the crash and been found washed up on shore by Sean McCullough. When she returned to Springfield, the clone was none too happy that Reva was back. The clone wanted to marry Josh herself, so she managed to keep Reva from Josh by continually locking her up someplace. Josh eventually learned Reva was alive and saved her.

Despondent, the clone took an overdose of an aging chemical and died of old age. But Josh and Reva's life had more complications to overcome when Annie came back with a new face and identity thanks to plastic surgery. Now calling herself Teri DeMarco, she dosed Josh with a drug that made him come on to Cassie. Unfortunately for Annie, the drug couldn't make Josh fall in love with her or hate Reva, but it did succeed in making him psychotic. So, when "Teri" staged an attack on herself and accused Josh, he was presumed guilty and arrested. This time it was Reva's turn to save Josh, and together they figured out the truth about Teri/Annie.

Just when it seemed Josh and Reva might be allowed to settle down to wedded bliss, Reva began being haunted by flashbacks from the five years when she was presumed dead. She and Josh traveled to the island of San Cristobel, where they learned that amnesiac Reva, going by the name of Catherine, had married Prince Richard, given birth to their son, then disappeared under mysterious circumstances. Once Richard caught sight of Reva, he wanted her back. . . .

Of Special Note: The actress who played Reva's clone as a young girl for nine episodes was Joie Lenz. "I was really surprised when I even got a call back for it, because I didn't think I looked anything like Kim at all," Lenz says. "They made me wear blue contacts and they lightened my hair a little bit, and I was surprised at how it worked." Lenz impressed the show's producers so much that they later hired her to take over the role of Michelle Bauer.

Real-Life Soap Opera: Kim Zimmer was born on February 2, 1955, in Grand Rapids, Michigan. After attending Hope College, she continued her professional training at the American Conservatory Theatre in San Francisco.

Her first roles in daytime were on *The Doctors,* where she played bad girl Nola Aldrich, and *One Life to Live,* where she was terrorist Echo DiSavoy. Although the roles may not have brought her instant stardom, they were an education.

"I had a life full of learning experiences working with actors such as Jada Rowland, David O'Brien, and Jim Pritchett," reminisces Zimmer. "And then the best teacher in the world, Erika Slezak. As well as Elizabeth Hubbard, who taught me how to remain active in big crowd scenes. When I asked Elizabeth her technique, she said, 'Darling, I just try to think of who just passed gas!' That kind of thing is invaluable."

Her career-changing role was Reva Shayne on *Guiding Light*. In 1990, however, dismayed at the direction the character was being taken, Zimmer, who is married to actor A. C. Weary, left the show.

"I had been playing the character consistently for six years and I was burned out. I had three children I wanted to spend time with and couldn't do it. When you work on a soap doing 40 to 50 pages of dialogue a day, it's hard. The fans get upset, but for health reasons, we have to take a mental break. Sort of let the computer chips get cleaned out so you can stuff in more material."

During her time away from daytime, Kim worked a bit in prime-time, including a recurring role on the short-lived primetime serial *Models, Inc.* She found quality roles for women scarce and soon realized how much she missed the soap world.

"In daytime, we make shit smell like roses," she said, creatively, at the time. "I've missed that."

Reva's reappearance was intended to be a twelve-week story arc, but due to fan response, Zimmer found herself back on the permanent cast list once again. She still occasionally gripes about Reva's storylines but seems content with her niche in the daytime entertainment world.

Awards and Accolades: Zimmer has earned three Daytime Emmy Awards for Outstanding Actress (1985, 1987, and 1990), as well as a *Soap Opera Digest* Award.

Feuds: It has long been rumored that Zimmer and Cynthia Watros, who played Annie, didn't get along, but Zimmer scoffs at the suggestion. "There is no truth to that at all!" she says, then adds, "I will honestly say that I am jealous of her because she's an incredible actress with the most perfect body in the world. And she's had the most wonderful material to perform this year. But we're buds and I knew her before she was on *Guiding Light*. If people want to believe that we don't get along, then let them believe it."

Div-o-Meter: 5—Despite her tenure and ability to command the stage when on it, Zimmer's onscreen character is too long-suffering and her offscreen demeanor too down-to-earth to climb past the middle echelons of divadom.

Guiding Light

Guiding Light holds the distinction of being the longest-running drama in show business history. Now in its forty-seventh season on television, the serial actually began sixty-two years ago on radio. Set in the Midwestern town of Springfield, the soap has revolved around the lives of the Bauer, Spaulding, Lewis, Reardon, and Cooper families.

Guiding Light premiered on radio in January 1937 and on CBS television on June 30, 1952.

The Div-o-Meter

OFF THE CHARTS

Susan
Lucci

TEN PLUS

Jeanne
Cooper

TEN

Linda
Dano

Susan
Flannery

Deidre
Hall

Beverlee
McKinsey

NINE

Elizabeth
Hubbard

Robin
Strasser

Jess
Walton

EIGHT

Eileen
Fulton

Hunter
Tylo

Marcy
Walker

Victoria
Wyndham

SEVEN

Patricia
Barry

Louise
Sorel

Ruth
Warrick

SIX

Lesley-Anne
Down

Erika
Slezak

FIVE

Marj
Dusay

Juliet
Mills

Kim
Zimmer

FOUR

Leslie
Charleson

Morgan
Fairchild

Anna
Stuart

THREE

TWO

ONE

Jaime Lyn
Bauer

Susan
Seaforth Hayes

Robin
Mattson

Julia
Barr

APPENDIX
Daytime Emmy Award Winners

*F*or many years, daytime programs and performers were not included on the Emmy ballots. The first year soap categories were included in the primetime ceremony was 1966. Beginning in 1974, daytime programs were honored in a ceremony of their own.

Following is the list of acting and show winners from the 1973–74 season to the present.

1973–74

Outstanding Daytime Drama Series: *The Doctors*

Best Actor in a Daytime Drama Series: Macdonald Carey (Tom, *Days of Our Lives*)

Best Actress in a Daytime Drama Series: Elizabeth Hubbard (Althea, *The Doctors*)

1974–75

Outstanding Daytime Drama Series: *The Young and the Restless*

Outstanding Actor in a Daytime Drama Series: Macdonald Carey (Tom, *Days of Our Lives*)

Outstanding Actress in a Daytime Drama Series: Susan Flannery (Laura, *Days of Our Lives*)

1975–76

Outstanding Daytime Drama Series: *Another World*

Outstanding Actor in a Daytime Drama Series: Larry Haines (Stu, *Search for Tomorrow*)

Outstanding Actress in a Daytime Drama Series: Helen Gallagher (Maeve, *Ryan's Hope*)

1976–77

Outstanding Daytime Drama Series: *Ryan's Hope*

Outstanding Actor in a Daytime Drama Series: Val Dufour (John, *Search for Tomorrow*)

Outstanding Actress in a Daytime Drama Series: Helen Gallagher (Maeve, *Ryan's Hope*)

1977–78

Outstanding Daytime Drama Series: *Days of Our Lives*

Outstanding Actor in a Daytime Drama Series: James Pritchett (Matt, *The Doctors*)

Outstanding Actress in a Daytime Drama Series: Laurie Heineman (Sharlene, *Another World*)

1978–79

Outstanding Daytime Drama Series: *Ryan's Hope*

Outstanding Actor in a Daytime Drama Series: Al Freeman (Ed, *One Life to Live*)

Outstanding Actress in a Daytime Drama Series: Irene Dailey (Liz, *Another World*)

Outstanding Supporting Actor in a Daytime Drama Series: Peter Hansen (Lee, *General Hospital*)

Outstanding Supporting Actress in a Daytime Drama Series: Suzanne Rogers (Maggie, *Days of Our Lives*)

1979–80

Outstanding Daytime Drama Series: *Guiding Light*

Outstanding Actor in a Daytime Drama Series: Douglass Watson (Mac, *Another World*)

Outstanding Actress in a Daytime Drama Series: Judith Light (Karen, *One Life to Live*)

Outstanding Supporting Actor in a Daytime Drama Series: Warren Burton (Eddie, *All My Children*)

Outstanding Supporting Actress in a Daytime Drama Series: Francesca James (Kelly, *All My Children*)

1980–81

Outstanding Drama Series: *General Hospital*

Outstanding Actor in a Daytime Drama Series: Douglass Watson (Mac, *Another World*)

Outstanding Actress in a Daytime Drama Series: Judith Light (Karen, *One Life to Live*)

Outstanding Supporting Actor in a Daytime Drama Series: Larry Haines (Stu, *Search for Tomorrow*)

Outstanding Supporting Actress in a Daytime Drama Series: Jane Elliot (Tracy, *General Hospital*)

1981–82

Outstanding Daytime Drama Series: *Guiding Light*

Outstanding Actor in a Daytime Drama Series: Anthony Geary (Luke, *General Hospital*)

Outstanding Actress in a Daytime Drama Series: Robin Strasser (Dorian, *One Life to Live*)

Outstanding Supporting Actor in a Daytime Drama Series: David Lewis (Edward, *General Hospital*)

Outstanding Supporting Actress in a Daytime Drama Series: Dorothy Lyman (Opal, *All My Children*)

1982–83

Outstanding Daytime Drama Series: *The Young and the Restless*

Outstanding Actor in a Daytime Drama Series: Robert S. Woods (Bo, *One Life to Live*)

Outstanding Actress in a Daytime Drama Series: Dorothy Lyman (Opal, *All My Children*)

Outstanding Supporting Actor in a Daytime Drama Series: Darnell Williams (Jesse, *All My Children*)

Outstanding Supporting Actress in a Daytime Drama Series: Louise Shaffer (Rae, *Ryan's Hope*)

1983–84

Outstanding Daytime Drama: *General Hospital*

Outstanding Actor in a Daytime Drama Series: Larry Bryggman (John, *As the World Turns*)

Outstanding Actress in a Daytime Drama Series: Erika Slezak (Viki, *One Life to Live*)

Outstanding Supporting Actor in a Daytime Drama Series: Justin Deas (Tom, *As the World Turns*)

Outstanding Supporting Actress in a Daytime Drama Series: Judi Evans (Beth, *Guiding Light*)

1984–85

Outstanding Daytime Drama Series: *The Young and the Restless*

Outstanding Actor in a Daytime Drama Series: Darnell Williams (Jesse, *All My Children*)

Outstanding Actress in a Daytime Drama Series: Kim Zimmer (Reva, *Guiding Light*)

Outstanding Supporting Actor in a Daytime Drama Series: Larry Gates (H. B., *Guiding Light*)

Outstanding Supporting Actress in a Daytime Drama Series: Beth Maitland (Traci, *The Young and the Restless*)

Outstanding Younger Actor in a Daytime Drama Series: Brian Bloom (Dusty, *As the World Turns*)

Outstanding Ingenue in a Daytime Drama Series: Tracey E. Bregman (Lauren, *The Young and the Restless*)

1985–86

Outstanding Daytime Drama Series: *The Young and the Restless*

Outstanding Actor in a Daytime Drama Series: David Canary (Adam/Stuart, *All My Children*)

Outstanding Actress in a Daytime Drama Series: Erika Slezak (Viki, *One Life to Live*)

Outstanding Supporting Actor in a Daytime Drama Series: John Wesley Shipp (Doug, *As the World Turns*)

Outstanding Supporting Actress in a Daytime Drama Series: Leann Hunley (Anna, *Days of Our Lives*)

Outstanding Younger Actor in a Daytime Drama Series: Michael Knight (Tad, *All My Children*)

Outstanding Ingenue in a Daytime Drama Series: Ellen Wheeler (Victoria/Marley, *Another World*)

1986-87

Outstanding Daytime Drama Series: *As the World Turns*

Outstanding Actor in a Daytime Drama Series: Larry Bryggman (John, *As the World Turns*)

Outstanding Actress in a Daytime Drama Series: Kim Zimmer (Reva, *Guiding Light*)

Outstanding Supporting Actor in a Daytime Drama Series: Gregg Marx (Tom, *As the World Turns*)

Outstanding Supporting Actress in a Daytime Drama Series: Kathleen Noone (Ellen, *All My Children*)

Outstanding Younger Actor in a Daytime Drama Series: Michael Knight (Tad, *All My Children*)

Outstanding Ingenue in a Daytime Drama Series: Martha Byrne (Lily, *As the World Turns*)

Outstanding Guest Performer in a Daytime Drama Series: John Wesley Shipp (Martin, *Santa Barbara*)

1987-88

Outstanding Daytime Drama Series: *Santa Barbara*

Outstanding Actor in a Daytime Drama Series: David Canary (Adam/Stuart, *All My Children*)

Outstanding Actress in a Daytime Drama Series: Helen Gallagher (Maeve, *Ryan's Hope*)

Outstanding Supporting Actor in a Daytime Drama Series: Justin Deas (Keith, *Santa Barbara*)

Outstanding Supporting Actress in a Daytime Drama Series: Ellen
Wheeler (Cindy, *All My Children*)

Outstanding Younger Actor in a Daytime Drama Series: Billy
Warlock (Frankie, *Days of Our Lives*)

Outstanding Ingenue in a Daytime Drama Series: Julianne Moore
(Frannie/Sabrina, *As the World Turns*)

1988–89

Outstanding Daytime Drama Series: *Santa Barbara*

Outstanding Actor in a Daytime Drama Series: David Canary
(Adam/Stuart, *All My Children*)

Outstanding Actress in a Daytime Drama Series: Marcy Walker
(Eden, *Santa Barbara*)

Outstanding Supporting Actor in a Daytime Drama Series: Justin
Deas (Keith, *Santa Barbara*)

Outstanding Supporting Actress in a Daytime Drama Series: Nancy
Lee Grahn (Julia, *Santa Barbara*) and Debbi Morgan (Angie, *All
My Children*)

Outstanding Younger Actor in a Daytime Drama Series: Justin Gocke
(Brandon, *Santa Barbara*)

Outstanding Younger Actress in a Daytime Drama Series: Kimberly
McCullough (Robin, *General Hospital*)

1989–90

Outstanding Daytime Drama Series: *Santa Barbara*

Outstanding Actor in a Daytime Drama Series: A Martinez (Cruz,
Santa Barbara)

Outstanding Actress in a Daytime Drama Series: Kim Zimmer
(Reva, *Guiding Light*)

Outstanding Supporting Actor in a Daytime Drama Series: Henry Darrow (Rafael, *Santa Barbara*)

Outstanding Supporting Actress in a Daytime Drama Series: Julia Barr (Brooke, *All My Children*)

Outstanding Juvenile Male in a Daytime Drama Series: Andrew Kavovit (Paul, *As the World Turns*)

Outstanding Juvenile Female in a Daytime Drama Series: Cady McClain (Dixie, *All My Children*)

1990–91

Outstanding Daytime Drama Series: *As the World Turns*

Outstanding Actor in a Daytime Drama Series: Peter Bergman (Jack, *The Young and the Restless*)

Outstanding Actress in a Daytime Drama Series: Finola Hughes (Anna, *General Hospital*)

Outstanding Supporting Actor in a Daytime Drama Series: Bernie Barrow (Louie, *Loving*)

Outstanding Supporting Actress in a Daytime Drama Series: Jess Walton (Jill, *The Young and the Restless*)

Outstanding Younger Actor in a Daytime Drama Series: Rick Hearst (Alan-Michael, *Guiding Light*)

Outstanding Younger Actress in a Daytime Drama Series: Anne Heche (Victoria/Marley, *Another World*)

1991–92

Outstanding Drama Series: *All My Children*

Outstanding Actor in a Daytime Drama Series: Peter Bergman (Jack, *The Young and the Restless*)

Outstanding Actress in a Daytime Drama Series: Erika Slezak (Viki, *One Life to Live*)

Outstanding Supporting Actor in a Daytime Drama Series: Thom Christopher (Carlo, *One Life to Live*)

Outstanding Supporting Actress in a Daytime Drama Series: Maeve Kinkead (Vanessa, *Guiding Light*)

Outstanding Younger Actor in a Daytime Drama Series: Kristoff St. John (Neil, *The Young and the Restless*)

Outstanding Younger Actress in a Daytime Drama Series: Tricia Cast (Nina, *The Young and the Restless*)

1992–93

Outstanding Drama Series: *The Young and the Restless*

Outstanding Actor in a Daytime Drama Series: David Canary (Adam/Stuart, *All My Children*)

Outstanding Actress in a Daytime Drama Series: Linda Dano (Felicia, *Another World*)

Outstanding Supporting Actor in a Daytime Drama Series: Gerald Anthony (Marco, *General Hospital*)

Outstanding Supporting Actress in a Daytime Drama Series: Ellen Parker (Maureen, *Guiding Light*)

Outstanding Younger Leading Actor in a Daytime Drama Series: Monti Sharp (David, *Guiding Light*)

Outstanding Younger Leading Actress in a Daytime Drama Series: Heather Tom (Victoria, *The Young and the Restless*)

1993–94

Outstanding Drama Series: *All My Children*

Outstanding Actor in a Daytime Drama Series: Michael Zaslow (Roger, *Guiding Light*)

Outstanding Actress in a Daytime Drama Series: Hillary B. Smith (Nora, *One Life to Live*)

Outstanding Supporting Actor in a Daytime Drama Series: Justin Deas (Buzz, *Guiding Light*)

Outstanding Supporting Actress in a Daytime Drama Series: Susan Haskell (Marty, *One Life to Live*)

Outstanding Younger Actor in a Daytime Drama Series: Roger Howarth (Todd, *One Life to Live*)

Outstanding Younger Actress in a Daytime Drama Series: Melissa Hayden (Bridget, *Guiding Light*)

1994–95

Outstanding Drama Series: *General Hospital*

Outstanding Actor in a Daytime Drama Series: Justin Deas (Buzz, *Guiding Light*)

Outstanding Actress in a Daytime Drama Series: Erika Slezak (Viki, *One Life to Live*)

Outstanding Supporting Actor in a Daytime Drama Series: Jerry ver Dorn (Ross, *Guiding Light*)

Outstanding Supporting Actress in a Daytime Drama Series: Rena Sofer (Lois, *General Hospital*)

Outstanding Younger Actor in a Daytime Drama Series: Jonathan Jackson (Lucky, *General Hospital*)

Outstanding Younger Actress in a Daytime Drama Series: Sarah Michelle Gellar (Kendall, *All My Children*)

1995–96

Outstanding Drama Series: *General Hospital*

Outstanding Actor in a Daytime Drama Series: Charles Keating (Carl, *Another World*)

Outstanding Actress in a Daytime Drama Series: Erika Slezak (Viki, *One Life to Live*)

Outstanding Supporting Actor in a Daytime Drama Series: Jerry ver Dorn (Ross, *Guiding Light*)

Outstanding Supporting Actress in a Daytime Drama Series: Anna Holbrook (Sharlene, *Another World*)

Outstanding Young Actor in a Daytime Drama Series: Kevin Mambo (Marcus, *Guiding Light*)

Outstanding Younger Actress in a Daytime Drama Series: Kimberly McCullough (Robin, *General Hospital*)

1996–97

Outstanding Drama Series: *General Hospital*

Outstanding Actor in a Daytime Drama Series: Justin Deas (Buzz, *Guiding Light*)

Outstanding Actress in a Daytime Drama Series: Jess Walton (Jill, *The Young and the Restless*)

Outstanding Supporting Actor in a Daytime Drama Series: Ian Buchanan (James, *The Bold and the Beautiful*)

Outstanding Supporting Actress in a Daytime Drama Series: Michelle Stafford (Phyllis, *The Young and the Restless*)

Outstanding Younger Actor in a Daytime Drama Series: Kevin Mambo (Marcus, *Guiding Light*)

Outstanding Younger Actress in a Daytime Drama Series: Sarah Brown (Carly, *General Hospital*)

1997–98

Outstanding Drama Series: *All My Children*

Outstanding Actor in a Daytime Drama Series: Eric Braeden (Victor, *The Young and the Restless*)

Outstanding Actress in a Daytime Drama Series: Cynthia Watros (Annie, *Guiding Light*)

Outstanding Supporting Actor in a Daytime Drama Series: Steve Burton (Jason, *General Hospital*)

Outstanding Supporting Actress in a Daytime Drama Series: Julia Barr (Brooke, *All My Children*)

Outstanding Younger Actor in a Daytime Drama Series: Jonathan Jackson (Lucky, *General Hospital*)

Outstanding Younger Actress in a Daytime Drama Series: Sarah Brown (Carly, *General Hospital*)

1998–99

Outstanding Drama Series: *General Hospital*

Outstanding Actor in a Daytime Drama Series: Anthony Geary (Luke, *General Hospital*)

Outstanding Actress in a Daytime Drama Series: Susan Lucci (Erica, *All My Children*)

Outstanding Supporting Actor in a Daytime Drama Series: Stuart Damon (Alan, *General Hospital*)

Outstanding Supporting Actress in a Daytime Drama Series: Sharon Case (Sharon, *The Young and the Restless*)

Outstanding Younger Actor in a Daytime Drama Series: Jonathan Jackson (Lucky, *General Hospital*)

Outstanding Younger Actress in a Daytime Drama Series: Heather Tom (Victoria, *The Young and the Restless*)

INDEX

About the Author

KATHLEEN TRACY is the author of *The Girl's Got Bite: The Unofficial Guide to Buffy's World* (Renaissance, 1998) and biographies of Ricky Martin, Kelsey Grammar, Drew Carey, Ellen DeGeneres, and Don Imus. An entertainment journalist for such magazines as *Globe, Film News International,* and *TV Week,* she is a member of the Television Critics Association and is accredited by the Motion Picture Association of America. She lives in Sherman Oaks, California.

Also available from Renaissance Books

The Ultimate Another World Trivia Book
by Gerard J. Waggett
ISBN: 1-58063-081-2 • $9.95

The Ultimate Days of Our Lives Trivia Book
by Gerard J. Waggett
ISBN: 1-58063-049-9 • $9.95

The Ultimate Young and the Restless Trivia Book
by Gerard J. Waggett
ISBN: 1-58063-145-2 • $9.95

From Soap Stars to Superstars: Celebrities Who Started Out in Daytime Drama
by Annette D'Agostino
ISBN: 1-58063-075-8 • $14.95

The Girl's Got Bite: An Unofficial Guide to Buffy's World
by Kathleen Tracy
ISBN: 1-58063-035-9 • $14.95

Party of Five: The Unofficial Companion
by Brenda Scott Royce
ISBN: 1-58063-000-6 • $14.95

That Lawyer Girl: An Unauthorized Guide to Ally's World
by A. C. Beck
ISBN: 1-58063-044-8 • $14.95

TO ORDER PLEASE CALL
1-800-452-5589